Cambridge Elements ☰

Elements in Public and Nonprofit Administration
edited by
Andrew Whitford
University of Georgia
Robert Christensen
Brigham Young University

COUNTRY SIZE AND PUBLIC ADMINISTRATION

Marlene Jugl
Bocconi University

CAMBRIDGE
UNIVERSITY PRESS

University Printing House, Cambridge CB2 8BS, United Kingdom

One Liberty Plaza, 20th Floor, New York, NY 10006, USA

477 Williamstown Road, Port Melbourne, VIC 3207, Australia

314–321, 3rd Floor, Plot 3, Splendor Forum, Jasola District Centre, New Delhi – 110025, India

103 Penang Road, #05–06/07, Visioncrest Commercial, Singapore 238467

Cambridge University Press is part of the University of Cambridge.

It furthers the University's mission by disseminating knowledge in the pursuit of education, learning, and research at the highest international levels of excellence.

www.cambridge.org
Information on this title: www.cambridge.org/9781009114110
DOI: 10.1017/9781009122887

First published 2022

A catalogue record for this publication is available from the British Library.

ISBN 978-1-009-11411-0 Paperback
ISSN 2515-4303 (online)
ISSN 2515-429X (print)

Country Size and Public Administration

Elements in Public and Nonprofit Administration

DOI: 10.1017/9781009122887
First published online: June 2022

Marlene Jugl
Bocconi University
Author for correspondence: Marlene Jugl, marlene.jugl@unibocconi.it

Abstract: Although countries differ tremendously in population size, comparative public administration has not considered this contextual factor systematically. This Element provides the most comprehensive theoretical and empirical account to date of the effects that country size has on the functioning of public administration. It synthesizes existing literature and develops a theoretical framework that distinguishes the effects of small, medium, and large country size on administrative structures, practices, and public service performance. Large states with larger administrations benefit from specialization but are prone to coordination problems, whereas small states experience advantages and disadvantages linked to multifunctionalism and informal practices. Midsize countries may achieve economies of scale while avoiding diseconomies of excessive size, which potentially allows for the highest performance. Descriptive and causal statistical analyses of worldwide indicators and a qualitative comparison of three countries, Luxembourg, the Netherlands, and Germany, demonstrate the various ways in which size matters for public administrations around the world.

This Element also has a video abstract: www.cambridge.org/jugl

Keywords: comparative public administration, context, economies of scale, small states, mixed methods

ISBNs: 9781009114110 (PB), 9781009122887 (OC)
ISSNs: 2515-4303 (online), 2515-429X (print)

Contents

1 Introduction

Countries differ tremendously in size. Today, independent countries vary from populations barely over 10,000, for example in Nauru and Tuvalu, to up to almost 1.4 billion in China. China is more than 100,000 times larger than the small Pacific island states. Even a less extreme comparison between the United States and Australia reveals that the former is about 13 times larger than the latter in terms of population size. These differences are considerable and have important, yet understudied, implications for public administration.

For example, public administrators in Luxembourg reason that "Luxembourg is very small; usually, everybody knows everybody" which allows for "relative direct short ways" of communication and "simplifies contacts and reaction time"[1] in the face of challenges. And yet, this rich but small country of roughly 600,000 inhabitants lacks the administrative resources to attend all meetings at the European Union (EU) level. Instead, Luxembourg's top officials need to prioritize and sometimes hand over their role and even voting rights to officials from Belgium, their midsize but considerably larger neighboring state (Thorhallsson 2000, 57). On the other hand, "a giant [government] system like India's has an inherent, inbuilt tendency to be cumbersome" (Lewis 1991, 368–69). The Covid-19 pandemic has revealed that larger and more fragmented administrative systems have more difficulties in adopting and coordinating a governmental response to a novel challenge (Bromfield and McConnell 2021; Kettl 2020; Toshkov, Yesilkagit, and Carroll 2021).

Despite large variations in country size and an increasing research focus on contextual factors, issues of size have received insufficient attention by scholars in public management and comparative public administration. The aim of this Element is threefold: first, to offer an overview of country size effects on public administration, especially at the central government level, second, to develop a research agenda around this emerging topic, and third, to provide detailed examples of comparative research techniques for studying contextual factors in PA. The following questions guide this Element: *How does size matter for the organization and functioning of public administration? What is the effect of size on administrative performance? Through which causal channels does size affect administrative performance? And how can size effects be studied empirically?*

There are important economies and diseconomies of scale, advantages and disadvantages of size, for administration. This Element develops a theoretical framework that integrates the effects of size on administrative structures, on practices, and ultimately on public service performance. I argue that there are

---

[1] Interviews conducted by the author in 2018, see Section 5.1.

mechanical-structural effects as well as cultural-attitudinal effects of size: larger states tend to have larger administrations that can specialize more at the individual, organizational, and system levels, which favors professionalism but comes with additional management costs. Smaller states, in contrast, can only afford administrations of smaller absolute size, which are typically restricted to certain key functions and characterized by multifunctional departments and multiple roles and tasks for individual public servants, which limits professionalization. Through a combination of these structural features of the administration and features of small societies, such as close personal ties and overlapping professional and private roles, small state administrations are dominated by informal practices. These practices can accelerate communication and coordination but also limit Weberian virtues like impartiality and professionalism. Specialized public administrations in large states, on the other hand, emphasize formal roles and rules more, which can have positive effects as well as negative ones such as silo thinking or bureaucratic politics.

Identifying these effects on structures and practices is of theoretical and practical importance, but it remains difficult to predict or assess their joint effects on public service performance. My more abstract and more provocative argument is that there is a golden mean or ideal country size for good administration. Regarding overall public service performance, medium-sized states have the potential for a virtuous combination of the "best of both worlds": a sufficient degree of specialization and professionalism with flexible and informal coordination practices, while avoiding the disadvantages of excessively large or small size. I argue that all else being equal, we should expect midsize states to achieve the highest levels of administrative performance, fulfill administrative tasks and deliver public services most effectively.

This introductory section sets the scene for later theoretical and empirical discussions. It situates the topic in the public administration literature, defines key concepts, and explains the Element's approach.

1.1 Locating the Argument in the Literature

Public administration research is becoming increasingly comparative and attentive to the role of context (Bertelli et al. 2020; Meier, Rutherford, and Avellaneda 2017; Ongaro, Gong, and Jing 2021; O'Toole Jr. and Meier 2014; van der Wal, van den Berg, and Haque 2021). Context can refer to a variety of factors beyond the direct control of public managers or policymakers. This includes external factors like political, cultural, and societal aspects, and contextual factors that are internal to the public organization including goal clarity, professionalism, and organizational culture. Context can have direct effects on the performance of public services or public organizations as well as indirect effects: it can moderate the relationship between a specific management structure, tool, or practice on the one hand and performance outcomes on the other (Ongaro, Gong, and Jing 2021; O'Toole Jr. and Meier 2017). For example, O'Toole and Meier (2017, 9) hypothesize that the dispersal of political power, a central element of a complex external environment, will have two effects. First, dispersal of political power will reduce the likelihood of administrative performance and program success because public managers must respond to more complex demands and expectations; this is the direct effect on performance. Second, in such a complex context of dispersed political power, the actions of public managers should have a greater impact on performance; this is the indirect effect on performance.

Studying context requires that researchers look at empirical cases or phenomena in different political, societal, and organizational contexts. This argument relates to Robert Dahl's (1947) classic claim that public administration should be studied from a comparative perspective (see also Pollitt 2011). Indeed, the debate on context has already sparked considerable progress in this regard, by openly encouraging and integrating studies from a variety of national backgrounds. However, public administration research continues to focus on large OECD countries such as the United States, the United Kingdom, or Germany- or the Netherlands, a medium-sized country. In particular, most public administration studies do not cover the full range of country sizes from very small to very large states, nor do they take size seriously. While scale issues receive some attention in terms of organizational size (Andrews, Beynon, and McDermott 2016; Bertels and Schulze-Gabrechten 2021; Jung and Kim 2014) or size of subnational units (Blom-Hansen, Houlberg, and Serritzlew 2014; Boyne 1995; Ostrom 1972), country size has been largely ignored as a contextual factor. Related studies in the field of economics on corruption (Knack and Azfar 2000; Xin and Rudel 2004), rule of law (Congdon Fors 2014; Olsson and Hansson 2011) or governance outcomes at large (Bräutigam and Woolcock 2001; Rose 2006) offer some insights, but their empirical results on country size effects are mixed and often lack convincing theoretical explanations.

Another strand of the literature focuses on the effects of *small* country size on governance and administration. Works in this vein are mostly theoretical (Randma-Liiv 2002; Randma-Liiv and Sarapuu 2019; Sarapuu 2010) or based on case studies (Corbett, Veenendaal, and Connell 2021; Dumont and Varone 2006). Randma-Liiv (2002) and Sarapuu (2010) aim at theoretical generalizations about small state administrations; their starting point is their experience as public administration scholars in a small state. Recently, they asked for more comparative research as "the knowledge on the impact of size is [still] ambiguous" (Randma-Liiv and Sarapuu 2019, 162). Based on qualitative case studies, Thorhalloooon (2000) analyzes how smallness shapes the foreign services of small European Union (EU) member states and their internal practices and performance in EU negotiations. Farrugia (1993) describes the problems of public administration in small developing countries. Recently, Corbett, Veenendaal, and Connell (2021) have compared coordination practices and challenges in six small states from various continents. The main shortcoming of these studies is that they do not include sufficient variance in size as the explanatory variable. They aim to derive generalizable arguments about size effects from single cases or a small number of small state cases. Although such analyses have some merits, especially those with a most-different systems design that distills the essence of diverse small state cases, they are limited. Largely descriptive approaches and an exclusive focus on small states do not offer enough analytical leverage to formulate generalizable claims about the effect of size as such.

This Element aims to fill some of these gaps in the literature. It conceptualizes country size not only as an independent variable but as a contextual meta factor, one that shapes administrative structures and practices as well as the social and political context in which public administration operates. This perspective combines structural-organizational aspects internal to the administration (Egeberg 1999) and cultural aspects in the administrations' environment (Bertelli et al. 2020; McDonnell 2017). The Element takes a macro-level perspective and focuses on "big questions" (Moynihan 2018), namely how size at the systems level affects the functioning of administration and how administrations can adapt to this macro-level factor. The theoretical framework also considers effects down to the meso level of institutions, organizations, and practices, and to the micro level of public administrators and their actions and attitudes. It demonstrates how size as a macro-level factor permeates administrative structures and behaviors at all levels (Roberts 2020). Importantly, every administrative system is affected by this contextual meta factor, not only those in small states. To study the effects of size, not smallness, and overcome the limitations of previous works, this Element compares countries of virtually all sizes, from Seychelles to China. Given the global perspective, the analyses span countries of different political, cultural, and economic contexts and distinguish size effects from these other important contextual factors.

Only a truly comparative perspective allows scholars and practitioners to fully understand the characteristics and constraints of their own national administrative system (Dahl 1947). Taking country size seriously as a contextual factor means rejecting one-size-fits-all solutions to public management. The Element's more practical goal is to raise awareness of the effects of country size among scholars and practitioners in national governments and international organizations. It invites the reader to reflect on how size structurally restricts public administration in their country or moderates the effect of management tools, and it suggests analytical approaches to study the effect of size. This should contribute to a better understanding and practice of public management and help to avoid the prescription or adoption of management structures or tools regardless of context or in contexts where they do not fit and undermine performance.

1.2 Conceptualizing Country Size

Before outlining the empirical approaches of the Element, it is necessary to clarify the key concept used here: country size. Far from being a merely technical matter of definition, the conceptualization of country size matters because concepts are important building blocks of research that link theory and empirics (Goertz 2006). While most people and researchers have an intuitive understanding of what constitutes a small or a large state, there is no agreement in the literature on a clear definition or operationalization. Essentially, country size refers to the size of an independent state, and the Oxford Dictionary defines "size" as the "relative extent of something; a thing's overall dimensions or magnitude; how big something is" (Stevenson 2015). While a magnitude can be objectively measured on a scale, the definition also refers to a relative extent. Size is an inherently relative and comparative concept. If only one country existed in the entire world, it would not be possible to indicate its size as small or large. One could measure its absolute magnitude in terms of population or area, but deducing from these indicators "how big" the country is would not be possible without a comparison. Since there are many countries in the world, labeling one as small implicitly means "smaller than others."

Country size can be conceptualized as a combination of several dimensions, most prominently population *(how many people?)*, area *(how big is the territory?)*, and resources, such as military, economic, or natural resources *(how powerful in economic or military terms?)* (Crowards 2002; Taylor 1969). In research practice, however, social scientists often employ more simplistic definitions and measures of country size. These definitions and measures vary between two poles. On one side, studies of a single case or a few cases (small N) tend to use relative, multidimensional concepts of size or smallness. These are often based on a qualitative assessment of several dimensions of size, resulting in categorical classification: a state is small or not. Focusing on one or a few cases allows scholars to consider multiple dimensions, including aspects of relative size compared to neighboring countries and aspects of identity (see, e.g., Campbell and Hall 2017; Gingrich and Hannerz 2017). It allows them to discuss at length how a specific country case fulfills these complex criteria for "smallness." On the other extreme, studies with a medium or large number of countries, especially quantitative studies in economics, require measures of country size that are quantifiable and easily comparable, most commonly utilizing population size (e.g. Alesina and Wacziarg 1998; Congdon Fors 2014) followed by area (Olsson and Hansson 2011).

Public administration and governance research often lie between these two extremes with a tendency to employ quantitative indicators of country size, primarily population size, but with a focus on cutoff points instead of a continuous scale (Streeten 1993; Thorhallsson 2000). For example, Randma-Liiv (2002, 375) uses a threshold of 2 million to define small states; Corbett, Veenendaal, and Connell (2021, 107) use 1 million; and other prominent cutoffs are at 1.5 and 3 million. Many authors admit that cutoff points or thresholds that separate small states from others (i.e., medium and large states) are inherently arbitrary and debatable (Panke 2010, 15; Taylor 1969, 116–17). The use of thresholds does not preclude a comparative perspective, although it often goes together with an exclusive focus on small states and disregard of larger ones. However, it predefines a *categorical* understanding of size, which means that a country can either be small or not according to a definition or cutoff, but it does not allow for degrees or gray areas. In contrast, Sarapuu and Randma-Liiv (2020, 56) have recently highlighted the *continuous* nature of country size, which is an important conceptual step toward a truly comparative study of size effects on public administration.

In this Element, I understand the size of a country primarily in terms of its society and inhabitants and measure it as the absolute size of its population. While I acknowledge that country size is multidimensional, the sociodemographic dimension of size (compared to the economic and geographic dimensions) matters most from a public administration perspective because population size is a proxy for the human resource pool, the complexity and number of social relations in society, and the diversity of citizens' and bureaucrats' identities and preferences. Because this sociodemographic dimension of size is at the heart of the arguments developed in this Element, population size is the simplest and most appropriate operationalization. I apply a continuous understanding of country size (from now on synonymous with population size) and avoid a priori cutoffs for small or large states in order to consider the full empirical variation of country sizes.

1.3 The Approach of This Element

To answer the guiding questions about size and its effects on public administration, this Element creates a bridge between different perspectives. The next section discusses arguments about the effects of country size on public administration. It reviews theoretical arguments and empirical findings from literature on small state and more "mainstream" public administration research. It integrates them to present a new, coherent theoretical framework that clearly distinguishes size effects on administrative structure, practice, and performance. In doing so, it provides an unprecedented level of theoretical depth and detail on the topic. Another theoretical innovation already alluded to is that size effects are not only conceived for small states but also for medium-sized and large ones. By explicitly theorizing ideal-typical medium and large states, this framework enables the application of the size argument to states and administrations that are not considered "small states." Given the extreme variation in country size globally and even among the OECD countries, the proposed framework explains why size effects should not only be a preoccupation for small states.

To illustrate the theoretical arguments and demonstrate the applicability of the framework, three empirical sections follow. Because no research method is perfect, the three empirical sections employ different methods that complement each other. In doing so, they provide examples of how comparative research techniques can be applied fruitfully to the study of contextual factors in public administration. This answers calls to combine different research methods and to design research in order to explicitly address questions about context (Ongaro, Gong, and Jing 2021, 7). The specific methodological challenges, advantages, and disadvantages are discussed for each method in a way that is intended to be accessible for scholars and practitioners with different methodological training and backgrounds.

Section 3 presents descriptive data on national administrative systems from a variety of sources to provide evidence for the relationship between country size and the size, structure, practices, and performance of the (central) public administration across countries and broad geographic regions. To investigate these indicators in relation to population size, the section employs scatter plots, correlations, and comparisons of group means. The variety of sources ensures broad coverage and allows for an overview of size and public administration across the globe. Given the novelty of the comparative study of size effects on public administration, this descriptive analysis provides original insights and the most comprehensive mapping of varieties of country size, administrative size, structure, practice, and performance of its kind.

Section 4 presents explanatory statistical analyses of the relationship between population size and performance, applying more advanced statistical techniques to the data introduced in the preceding section. The section explains the motivation and rationale behind the modeling strategies: in short, a random-effect within-between model isolates the between-country effect of the sluggish population size variable, and an instrumental variable approach serves as a causal identification strategy. Based on a global sample of countries, the analysis reveals a robust inverse U-shaped relation, meaning that all else being equal, midsize states achieve the highest levels of performance. This relation is particularly marked among democracies.

Section 5 adopts a qualitative approach and compares three country cases based on a "most similar systems" design: it presents empirical case studies of public administration in Luxembourg (small), the Netherlands (medium), and Germany (large), which vary primarily in terms of country size but share many other characteristics. Based on government documents, academic literature, and original field research, the section describes the countries' administrative systems, structural and organizational particularities, systematic challenges, and performance and discusses how size affects these aspects. This section provides a more hands-on perspective on size effects, what difference size variation can make, and how size-based challenges can be addressed. As such, this section should be particularly relevant for practitioners.

While the three sections can be understood as separate empirical approaches to study size effects on public administration, they are constituent parts of the Element's larger mixed-methods strategy. Mixed methods (Mele and Belardinelli 2019), or the combination of methods for data collection and analysis, are used for two reasons. The first reason is to triangulate the findings and increase the validity of the results. The second reason is to gain a multilevel understanding of the phenomenon: How much of global variation in public administration practice and performance can be explained by size, and how and through which channels do size effects play out in individual countries? To form an integrated study, several "connecting points" (Mele and Belardinelli 2019, 337) link the different types of data and analysis in this Element. The research questions in this introductory section and the integration of findings in the concluding section form a bracket that integrates the empirical analyses. The theoretical framework helps align the analyses in Sections 3 and 5 along the dimensions of administrative structure, practice, and performance, while Section 4 focuses only on the performance dimension. In particular, different data sources and analytical techniques are used to respond to the same research questions and explore the same dimensions of administrative systems. Section 5 in itself combines data sources, including documents, indicators and interviews, and qualitative analytical techniques, namely within-case and between-case analysis. A complementary connecting point is that different analytical strategies are also applied to similar data sources. For example, the same performance indicator on Government Effectiveness is analyzed with descriptive statistics in Section 3, with causal statistical methods in Section 4, and as one among many data points in the qualitative analysis in Section 5. Finally, the selection of the three qualitative cases in Section 5 builds on the quantitative "mapping" of the global distributions of country size and on previous findings from the quantitative analyses.

The final section discusses conclusions and outlines a research agenda. I suggest for future research to examine size effects in understudied settings such as developing or nondemocratic countries and to explore the implications of size effects for policy making and substantive policy outcomes. Considerations about the advantages of small states and how they thrive despite limited resources may contribute to a better understanding of government success in a turbulent and increasingly complex world.

2 Theoretical Framework

Although several authors have identified different country size effects in public administration, there is no comprehensive and systematic theoretical account of these effects. This section addresses this gap by outlining an original theoretical framework that summarizes how different country sizes – small, medium, and large – affect the structures, practices, and performance of national public administration. This advances the literature about country size and public administration by synthesizing existing arguments and by formulating explicit theoretical expectations for medium-sized and large countries as well.

So far, the small state literature has neglected larger states as the implicit "other" with its focus on small states' administrative characteristics and challenges; whereas mainstream public administration treats medium and larger states as the implicit norm. My aim is to integrate both and make size effects explicit across the range of country sizes. Medium and larger states are not merely a mirror image of small states, defined by the absence of small-state characteristics. We should characterize large states by what they are rather than by what they are not. It is worth reemphasizing that I do not formulate empirical cutoffs or thresholds for small or large states *a priori*, although these labels (small, medium, and large) are central in the theoretical argument. Rather, I employ them as theoretical labels and theoretical ideal types. In this section, I do not specify to which empirical cases these arguments apply. It is an empirical question what a midsize state is, and at which population size the "golden mean" for administrative performance is reached. I tackle these empirical questions in Section 4.

The theoretical framework should be read with two qualifications in mind. First, it works under a *ceteris paribus* assumption. This assumption is often fundamental in comparative research, and it means that relations or effects that are expressed in theoretical or empirical terms only hold if all other factors are equal. In the context of this Element, this means that the arguments about size effects on administrative structure, practices, and performance should only be observable in a group of countries with similar levels of wealth, political systems, and political-administrative cultures and welfare systems. Characteristics pertaining to political, cultural, and social context should be similar because otherwise they could confound or outweigh the effect of country size. This Element does not claim that country size is the most important determinant or explanation of variation in administrative practice and performance. In a global comparison, income or GDP per capita explains a great deal of variation in public service performance. Country size is one of several determinants that drive the variation of bureaucracies across countries. In order to focus on this single factor, others must be held constant. This is an important caveat readers should keep in mind when comparing the theoretical arguments in this section with empirical cases of small, medium, or large states familiar to them. Later sections employ two empirical techniques to hold such factors constant: control variables in the quantitative analyses in Section 4 and theory-based case selection holding other important factors as constant as possible in Section 5.

A second and related qualification is that the arguments advanced are probabilistic rather than deterministic. They should not be interpreted as an eternal truth that applies in every single case, which would imply a deterministic understanding of a certain country size necessarily leading to a certain outcome. Instead, the expected size effects should apply as a tendency. A single case that is not fully congruent with the argument is not sufficient to invalidate the argument entirely, as long it holds for the majority of cases or "on average." My understanding of country size effects is also probabilistic. If a fictitious state "A" has a population of 0.5 million and "B" has 3.5 million, both are small, but state A is closer to the theoretical ideal type of a small state and is a clearer empirical manifestation of the concept of smallness. The continuous understanding of size comes with a probabilistic understanding of what a smaller or larger state entails. I presume that a country that is smaller than another *tends* more strongly to display the characteristics of smallness described in the literature (Benedict 1966, 1967; Gingrich and Hannerz 2017; Lowenthal 1987).

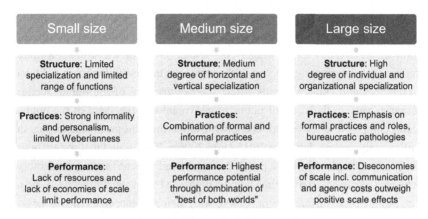

Figure 1 Theoretical framework

The theoretical framework is summarized in Figure 1. Each of the following subsections explains one part of the framework: the effects of different country sizes on administrative structures, on administrative practices, and on overall public service performance.

2.1 Size Effects on Administrative Structure

Economies of scale in public administration are based on two underlying ideas: first, per capita, fixed costs for bureaucratic institutions and public goods and services decrease with the number of citizens or taxpayers (Alesina and Wacziarg 1998, 308; Tullock 1969, 19–21). Second, a larger size of a firm, government agency, or jurisdiction allows specialization within and between organizations and for individual employees to fully develop specialized skills (Andrews and Boyne 2009; Blau 1970, 204, 210; Blom-Hansen, Houlberg, and Serritzlew 2014; Boyne 1995, 214–15; Ostrom 1972, 489). For large states, this means that all else being equal, they tend to have lower per capita costs of public administration (Alesina and Spolaore 2005, 172). These lower costs, together with more diverse demand for public goods, services, and regulation in larger states, lead to larger bureaucracies. The central point here is that large countries have larger public administrations in absolute numbers. Gerring and Maguire (2014, 8, 78) confirm this relation empirically and show that the number of government employees is positively and significantly associated with population size in about 120 countries between 1985 and 2005. In their sample, population size alone explains about 80 percent, a very large part, of variation in government employees. Likewise, Thorhallson (2006, 20) reports a strong correlation between population size and the number of bureaucrats in EU countries' foreign services, a national-level administration whose size is linked to resources rather than internal demands from citizens.

These numbers reflect that population size is systematically linked to the *absolute* size of public administration. Here, one may ask about the role of political preferences for a "bigger" or "leaner" state or a country's welfare tradition for determining the size of the state. Yet these differences in political preferences and choices mostly affect the *relative* size of the public sector: countries vary in the share of public employment and the share of the public sector compared to the overall economy. Comparing European countries in an earlier analysis with data from 2015 (Jugl 2020b, 79), I found that the share of government employment as a percent of total employment varies considerably between Germany (10.6%), the United Kingdom (16.4%), and France (21.4%). Yet, despite these differences in relative size, their absolute size remains large, ranging from 4.5 million (Germany) to 5.9 million (France) government employees. These absolute numbers are several orders of magnitude above those of very small European countries: although typically classified as belonging to different administrative traditions and welfare regime types, small European states with populations below 3 million have consistently smaller public administrations between 50,300 (Luxembourg) and 305,000 (Lithuania) government employees. In short, the *absolute* size of the public sector and public administration is driven above all by a country's population size, and political choices modify this only to a marginal degree. The following discussion on differences in public administration in small, medium, and large states builds primarily on this difference in absolute size.

The larger *absolute* size of the administrative system in large countries allows for more specialization at the system (macro) level. With more bureaucrats in each organization (agency, department, etc.) and in each organizational unit than in small states, it also allows for more specialization at the organizational (meso) and individual (micro) levels. Larger bureaucratic organizations tend to be more specialized internally, so they can adequately address most topics and tasks that arise. Specialization can be vertical and territorial through federalism and decentralization, as in the cases of India or the United States. Specialization can also be thematic and horizontal through the division of labor and tasks between and within government organizations (see Egeberg 1999). In larger administrative systems and units, individual bureaucrats can also specialize more on certain tasks; receive advanced training, which requires a "critical mass" of participants with similar specialization; and develop and use their skills to the fullest (Rainey and Steinbauer 1999, 22).

However, the large size of an administration comes at a cost; it creates a structural-mechanical disadvantage. With a fixed maximum span of control in a hierarchical system, an increase in employees implies an increase in the number of superiors overseeing these employees, and since these superiors have to be monitored or instructed in turn, an additional layer of superiors or managers is required (Blau 1970, 213–14; Urwick 2003 [1937], 54–60). The larger an administrative organization, the more the need for organizational levels and management staff, which increases the share of internal administration. An extensive literature argues that overall administrative costs increase exponentially with organizational size (Andrews and Boyne 2009, 742; Downs 1967, 130–31, 141; Jung 2013, 668; Williamson 1967, 127). Parts of these exponentially growing barriers to administrative effectiveness are communication costs, or when information is condensed and partly lost at every organizational level it travels up the hierarchy. Another part is agency costs: when commands are specified and interpreted repeatedly at several levels down the hierchy, this can distort their meaning (Downs 1967, 50, 76, 118, 134; Treisman 2007, 63–73; Tullock 1969, 25). I expect that these costs occur not only within large public organizations but also at the overall level of large, specialized administrative systems (Bouckaert, Peters, and Verhoest 2010, 13–33; e.g., on India, see Lewis 1991, 368–71). These diseconomies of scale are the downside of large countries' specialized bureaucracies and limit public service effectiveness.

The link between country size and macro-level specialization has received empirical attention from political scientists who refer to specialization as the "distribution of power" between government organizations and levels. Bernauer and Vatter (2017, 265–67, 270–71) find that population size and area systematically affect vertical power distribution in continental European countries. Hooghe and Marks (2013, 191–94) find that population size outperforms area at explaining levels of regional or subnational authority in advanced democracies. They use the term regional authority to refer to the exercise of governing power by general-purpose governments below the national level. Hooghe and Marks' (2013, 194) results explain, for example, the high degrees of governing authority exercised by the US states and by the *Länder* in Germany with these countries' large population size in international comparison. In short, larger states tend to be more vertically specialized. Gerring and colleagues (2018) bring institutions of horizontal and vertical power distribution together in a "general theory of power concentration" and examine the relation with the size of a polity (Gerring, Maguire, and Jaeger 2018, 491, 494). They argue that power is diffused in larger polities in order, first, to increase efficiency in light of a heterogeneous population that is divided into a larger number of groups than in smaller states and, second, to solve problems of trust that occur when governments rule over many people (Gerring, Maguire, and Jaeger 2018, 496–98). In a series of regression models, they estimate the effect of population size on 15 measures of horizontal and vertical power concentration across more than 100 years and 100 countries and conclude that population size is the only generalizable cause of power diffusion or concentration. Applied to public administrations, these studies support the argument that large size goes hand in hand with more institutional specialization and diffusion of task responsibilities among several tiers and organizations.

From the perspective of small states, ideas about economies of scale translate into a double disadvantage. First, relative to their population size, they tend to have a "disproportionately large" (Randma-Liiv 2002, 378) public sector with high per capita costs (Alesina and Wacziarg 1998). At the same time, mirroring their small population, they have a small absolute number of bureaucrats compared to larger states (Thorhallsson 2006, 20). This small absolute size of public administration puts important limits on its structure and functioning. Moreover, it has been argued that small states are less heterogeneous, for example, in terms of socioeconomic groups, professions, ethnicities, and life-styles (Dahl and Tufte 1973, 30–31, 40; Gerring, Maguire, and Jaeger 2018, 496) but also physical environments, which reduces the demand for specialized public services and regulations. In terms of administrative structure, limited absolute size and limited demand restrict the range of administrative functions covered as well as the degree of specialization (Jugl 2020b).

A limited range of functions results directly from small absolute size. Limited resources, resulting from a small number of taxpayers and bureaucrats, do not allow public administration in small states to cover all potential tasks and provide all public goods and services as administrations in larger states do. Limited resources constrain political decision-makers and public managers to prioritize certain tasks or interests as "islands of excellence" (McDonnell 2017; Panke 2010, 204; Thorhallsson 2000, 55–59) and leave others more or less aside (Sarapuu 2010, 34). Whereas small states "need to address their security and international relations, their economic, environmental, education and health policies as well as their system of justice" (Randma-Liiv and Sarapuu 2019, 167) as any other state and provide the basic public goods and services citizens expect, they often lack resources to tackle less fundamental tasks. An example of a seemingly less fundamental, frequently omitted task in small states is the collection, processing, and publication of detailed statistical data. This poses a serious problem for comparative social science research because it often leads to the omission of small state observations and their experience from comparative studies.

The second structural effect of smallness is limited specialization: the smaller a country and its administration are, the less it can specialize internally (Dahl and Tufte 1973, 36–39; Thorhallsson 2000, chapter 3). This results in a number of structural features identified in studies of small state administrations, which range from the macro level of state organization down to the micro level of the individual bureaucrat (Jugl 2020b).

- *Limited vertical specialization at the state level:* At the macro level, limited resources and a small absolute size of the administration typically lead to a centralized organization of the state (Randma-Liiv and Sarapuu 2019, 173–74). In Hooghe and Marks' study, Luxemburg, Malta, and Iceland are by far the smallest countries in terms of population, all three below 1 million, and they have the lowest levels of subnational authority: "Iceland, for example, has an intermediate government (*landsvæðun*) that exists only as a statistical category" (Hooghe and Marks 2013, 193). Decentralization is often discussed in larger states as a way to bring politics and administration closer to the people and to adapt policies to subnational preferences and tastes (Alesina and Spolaore 2005; Diamond and Tsalik 1999), but the same vertical differentiation would undermine administrative effectiveness in small states by dividing resources and multiplying problems related to resource scarcity (Jugl 2019, 129). This is why we rarely see anything other than centralized, unitary states in small countries. Veenendaal (2014, 191) presents a rare counter-example, the case of Palau that retains a federalist system with division of power and responsibilities despite having fewer than 20,000 inhabitants. One of his interviewees summarizes the absurdity of oversized and ineffective administrative units: "How can you have thirty-five people staying in Sonsorol [one of 16 Palauan states] and they are considered as a state?" (Veenendaal 2014, 191). Palau is an example that deviates from the size effects theorized here, and Veenendaal explains this with historical heritage and desire to copy the US federal system, without regard for the vast difference in country size. The example reminds us that other factors, here historical and geographic aspects, also matter for government structure, yet they may result in structures that are a bad fit for the given country size.
- *Limited horizontal specialization at the central government level:* National governments in small states tend to be divided into fewer portfolios or ministries than in medium-sized and larger states. For example, a minister from small Estonia joked about feeling like a super minister at EU meetings because his portfolio covers broad policy fields, from health to labor, social security, and equal opportunities, which are divided into several ministries in larger states (Sarapuu 2010, 30). In the case of small Luxembourg, the number of distinct ministries is not particularly small but "multiple portfolios are in the hands of a small number of ministers" (Dumont and Varone 2006, 65). Both examples are variations of the same phenomenon that is best described as "polyvalence," a term that comes from sociology and has gained wider attention in small-state research (Benedict 1967, 6–9; Gingrich and Hannerz 2017, 18–19). Polyvalence means that individuals in small societies typically occupy several roles in the professional and private realm,

and because of smallness and social proximity these roles overlap, thus creating a dense web of relations (Katzenstein 1985, 89; Sutton 1987, 15). The polyvalence and multifunctionalism we see at the head of government ministries or departments equally apply to whole administrative organizations, which tend to be less numerous and less functionally specialized than in larger states.

- *Limited vertical and horizontal specialization at the organizational level:* In small states, there also tends to be less hierarchical and functional differentiation *within* each administrative organization, that is, within each ministry, department, or agency. These organizations have flatter internal hierarchies and fewer units at each hierarchical level. Moreover, units at the working level are typically responsible for more topics and tasks and are accordingly less specialized than their counterparts in larger states. This level of specialization has been largely overlooked by the small state literature. It became apparent, though, in a comparison (Jugl 2020b) of the organizational charts of the interior ministries in Estonia and Germany, with Germany being more than 50 times larger in terms of population. Below the political top management level, Estonia's ministry counted 3 divisions with 3 to 6 working units each, while the German ministry consisted of more divisions (14 in total and at least 7 that cover the same policy areas as the Estonian ministry). In addition, the German ministry had a further level of subdivisions (2 to 3 per division) and a considerably higher number of working units (5 to 8 per subdivision). The stark difference in internal specialization is obvious in the organization charts.

- *Limited vertical and horizontal specialization at the individual level:* Limited specialization at the level of the individual public servant is a key feature and challenge in small state administrations (Farrugia 1993). It is particularly visible for top-level bureaucrats, whose positions are characterized by horizontal and vertical polyvalence. With horizontal polyvalence, I mean that individual top-level bureaucrats cover several thematic policy issues. Vertical polyvalence refers to the fulfillment of different types of tasks; these may range from the top level, for example, advising the minister on strategic policy issues (for the overlap of political and administrative functions see Randma-Liiv 2002, 379), down to the street level, for example, dealing with the day-to-day challenges related to the implementation of a specific policy or with its beneficiaries. Vertical polyvalence occurs simply because there are fewer people to delegate to.

Most of the arguments reviewed here are based on a continuous understanding of country size and size effects: the larger a state, the more the possibility of structural specialization. This perspective allows us to derive expectations for midsize states that are located between the two extremes of small and large states: medium-sized states should have a medium number of public employees and a medium-sized central administration in absolute terms and compared to other states. This should allow for a mid-level degree of horizontal and vertical specialization. In midsize countries, more differentiation at the state, organizational, and individual levels should be possible than in small states, but we should expect less extreme forms of decentralization, organizational differentiation, and individual specialization than in very large ones.

2.2 Size Effects on Administrative Practices

Good public administration practice is often defined in terms of Weberian virtues: professional, rule-based, and merit-based (Evans and Rauch 1999; Nistotskaya and Cingolani 2016; Rauch and Evans 2000). What may be less well known among public administration scholars is that Max Weber himself explicitly linked this idea of bureaucracy with country size. He argued that bureaucracy has developed "far more comprehensively [in larger states] than in the city states . . . for the basis of bureaucratization has always been a certain development of administrative tasks, both quantitative and qualitative" (Weber 1978 [1922], 968–69). To attain a professional public service and administrative practice, a certain size of the country and administration that allows for specialization are necessary. Vice versa, sociologists have suggested that since a larger number of bureaucrats is more difficult to monitor, country size should be positively related to hierarchical steering and control mechanisms that are characteristic of bureaucracies (Kiser and Baer 2005, 232; Kiser and Schneider 1994). In the same vein, public administration and organization scholars have argued that the proportion of internal administration, management, and monitoring increases exponentially with organizational size (Andrews and Boyne 2009, 742; Downs 1967, 130–31; Jung 2013, 668; Williamson 1967, 127).

Among the characteristics of bureaucracies that Weber (1978 [1922], 956–58) mentions, three are central to good administrative procedures and practices: they should be professional, merit-based, and rule-based. Professionalization is based on specialization (Egeberg 1999), which was discussed in the previous section about administrative structure. A certain size of administration, scope of administrative tasks, and degree of specialization require capable, skilled, and dedicated public servants to carry out clearly defined, specialized roles. The result at the micro level is public servants who pursue a clearly defined and specialized, formal role assigned to them as their job and main source of income. The higher the degree of formal specialization, the more these officials need "thorough training in a field of specialization" (Weber 1978 [1922], 958), and advanced professional training requires a "critical mass" of participants with similar specialization (Rainey and Steinbauer 1999, 22; Wilson 1989). A critical mass of bureaucrats – as in large administrations – is also essential for the formation of professional associations and a distinct bureaucratic identity, which enhance the virtuous separation of interests between politicians and bureaucrats and shields the administration from excessive political interference (Dahlström, Lapuente, and Teorell 2012; Rainey and Steinbauer 1999, 22). Through these channels, size and specialization foster bureaucratic professionalism (see also Rauch and Evans 2000, 51–53).

Professionalization is closely linked with the second Weberian feature that is central to our discussion: merit-based recruitment and advancement. Merit-based recruitment shapes internal administrative practices because it prevents patronage and political interference and instead ensures the primacy of professional decision making based on professional skills and knowledge (Evans and Rauch 1999; Nistotskaya and Cingolani 2016; Dahlström, Lapuente, and Teorell 2012). Besides a demand-side argument, we can also expect large states to have a highly professional administration (under the ceteris paribus assumption) because the supply of professionally educated candidates is higher in larger societies, which allows for the recruitment of more qualified officials. Merit-based recruitment is achieved through a formal recruitment process, which may differ in practice, but must follow transparent rules.

This links to the third important feature: rule-based administrative practices. Weber argues that the management of a bureaucratic organization should follow "general rules, which are more or less stable, more or less exhaustive" (Weber 1978 [1922], 958). Internal rules prescribe and codify specific administrative practices, define the criteria for administrative decisions, and ensure impartiality. Again, such rules become more important the larger the organization or administrative system, because with increasing size the political or administrative leadership cannot supervise every individual public servant but relies on formal rules to ensure uniform administrative behavior.

In sum, a large country size can foster the establishment of formal professional roles and formal rules for recruitment, administrative procedures, and decision making. This is based on a well-known general feature of human organizations: the larger they become, the more formal rules, roles, and hierarchies are needed to steer them (see Durkheim 1893; Gellner 1973). Personal ties and relations, on the other hand, should matter less in larger states because the sheer size of administrative organizations and the administrative system requires formalized roles and procedures and makes personal relations between a large number of officials (and politicians) less likely.

Besides these three "Weberian virtues," the public administration literature increasingly highlights the downsides and negative side effects of specialized organizations and bureaucratic structures. Since the need and opportunity for specialization, professionalization, and formalization is higher in larger states and administrations, I also expect these pathologies to be more likely in large states. The archetypical pathology of bureaucratic organizations is silo thinking (Bach and Wegrich 2019, 11–13). It results from structural specialization, which forces units or individuals to think only about a subset of collective goals, which may be in conflict with other subsets (Egeberg 1999; Hood 1974). Clearly defined tasks focus the attention of the administrative organization and public servants, and administrative procedures are formalized and fine-tuned to fulfill these specific tasks. However, such specialized structures and formalized procedures create problems for thinking beyond this "silo" and for coordinating with other organizational units and organizations (Cerulo 2006).

Specialization and professionalization can also result in overly homogeneous groups of public servants with similar (professional) backgrounds, who share similar perspectives on problems and policy solutions and may overlook alternatives. The sociologists Fligstein, Stuart Brundage, and Schultz (2017) have demonstrated how these pathologies have long prevented the American Federal Reserve (Fed) from recognizing the emerging economic crisis of 2008, which has delayed a government response. In particular, homogeneous professional backgrounds among the highly educated members of the Fed's Federal Open Market Committee led to the dominance of macroeconomic frames in meetings, which prevented perception of the crucial connection between the housing sector and the financial system. In this case, specialization led to a professional bias in administrative practices and ultimately impeded the achievement of overarching policy goals, here economic stability.

Another pathology of specialization, besides these structural-mechanical ones, relates to organizational identities. The literature on bureaucratic politics (Wilson 1989; t'Hart and Wille 2012) argues that large and bureaucratic administrations nurture distinct and conflicting identities among different public organizations. The larger and the more specialized administrative organizations are and the more organizations compete for political attention and resources – all of which I expect in a larger state – the more they will take on distinct identities that can result in rivalries and conflict. Conflicting organizational identities can impede identification with common goals and joint action and lead to practices such as bureaucratic politics and reputation-seeking, which hamper the exchange of information and insights (Bach and Wegrich 2019, 15–18; McDonnell 2017, 480). Wilson (1989) famously argued that specialized administrative organizations with distinct professional norms are primarily interested in protecting their turf and autonomy, which "can and often does involve eliminating or otherwise coping with the threats posed by rivals" (Wilson 1989, 181). However, his observations are rooted in the US context, a large country and administrative system with ample specialization and fragmentation, where "a half dozen other agencies" (Wilson 1989, 181) are responsible for a similar task, which likely leads to conflict and makes coordination necessary but at the same time extremely difficult. Along these lines, Yasuda (2015, 750–51) links turf wars in the Chinese bureaucracy to the country's sheer size and the scale of policy problems. In the case of this gigantic country, Yasuda shows that rivalries between administrative organizations play a central role in administrative practice and regulatory failure in the area of food safety.

In fact, most of the literature on bureaucratic pathologies or "administrative diseases" (Hood 1974) focuses on the context of relatively large countries without explicitly acknowledging size as a crucial precondition to specialization, bureaucratization, and these pathologies. In the framework of this Element, these pathologies are conceptualized as practices that result, more or less unintendedly, from the large size of a country and its administrative system.

Besides silo thinking and bureaucratic politics, another disadvantage of large and specialized administrative systems is that they undermine the coherence between public servants' tasks at the micro-level and, more general, meso-level organizational goals (Rainey and Jung 2015, 74–76). If highly specialized tasks and practices become too monotonous or seemingly insignificant, individual bureaucrats may lose motivation and perform less well (Grindle 2012, 13, 51–52). Finally, from the perspective of citizens and service users, strongly formalized procedures may appear overly complex and responsibilities may be unclear, all feeding into the experience of "administrative burden" (Moynihan, Herd, and Harvey 2015), red tape, or "over-organization" (Hood 1974, 443).

How do these considerations play out at the other end of the size continuum? In short, I argue that public administrations in small states are characterized by less Weberian and more informal practices, which can have positive and negative effects. Randma-Liiv (2002) suggests that characteristics of small state administrations, including constraints on economic and human resources, make it difficult to copy Weberian ideas of universality and formal, rule-based practices from large to small states. As argued before, small size does not allow for much specialization, which is the precondition for professional and rule-based practices in Weber's sense. Let us consider the effects of this observation on practices at the micro, meso, and macro levels of small state administrations.

At the micro level, limited specialization of individuals results in the accumulation of roles (polyvalence) and potentially conflicting tasks, as mentioned previously. In practice, this leads to limited knowledge and skills in each area and task. Farrugia (1993, 222–24) argued that this is an important source of frustration and stress for the individual bureaucrat in small developing countries and that it also hampers the professionalism of the entire administration. The lack of professional skills is aggravated when bureaucracies can recruit only from a very small pool of professional personnel, which is often the case in small developing countries (Jugl et al. 2021; Randma-Liiv 2002, 377–82). On a more positive note, these environmental pressures allow individual bureaucrats, especially in senior positions, to be "not only role-takers but also role-makers" (Sarapuu and Randma-Liiv 2020, 61). Job descriptions are often adapted to the available candidate rather than the other way around. Individuals matter more than formal roles, and individuals can have extensive discretion in an organization made up of few(er) individuals. Although this deviates from Weber's ideal-typical bureaucratic practices, it seems appropriate or unavoidable in the small state context with scarce human resources.

Another positive effect of individual polyvalence is that it can strengthen job motivation. Role accumulation allows a larger share of public servants to interact with citizens and beneficiaries and directly serve the public interest, which reinforces task significance and motivation (Anderson and Stritch 2016, 212–13; Harari et al. 2017, 80). Individual and organizational polyvalence also facilitate a generalist orientation (Jann and Wegrich 2019; Thorhallsson 2000, 81) among small states' bureaucrats. They limit the ambiguity and divergence between general policy goals and the subsets of specific operative goals that Hood (1974) referred to. Especially among senior public servants who make policy-relevant decisions, polyvalence helps to think broadly about a problem and consider "the big picture" (Sarapuu and Randma-Liiv 2020, 58), attenuating silo thinking.

At the meso level, less specialization between and within administrative organizations facilitates coordination (see Egeberg 1999). Organizational polyvalence means that each organization or unit combines several tasks and responsibilities, but there is hardly any overlap between organizations and units (compare with Wilson's quote about the United States above). Clearer responsibilities and fewer organizational actors make interorganizational coordination easier. And organizations with fewer members can be managed in flatter hierarchies and with less formalized coordination mechanisms. Thorhallsson (2000, 81–84), for example, observes in EU negotiations that negotiators of small member states have direct contact with policy experts from different ministries in their country and even with the government ministers, in stark contrast with practices in larger member states. Thorhallsson (2000, 81, 90) also reports that negotiators from small states – who are high-level public servants – have more room for maneuver than their counterparts from larger states, who must represent sometimes delicate compromises between different domestic organizations and are constrained by internal procedures. This also illustrates the earlier argument that individuals play a more central role in decision making in small state administrations. Another example of limited formal control mechanisms relates to performance management. Small state administrations face particular challenges when adopting performance management practices, which are prominent in "mainstream" public administration theory and practice. Sarapuu and Randma-Liiv (2020, 59) argue that because small states' administrative organizations and public servants are multifunctional, their performance is difficult to measure in a standardized way, which is a prerequisite for performance management. In sum, with regard to everyday administrative practice and decisions, small size puts less of a distance – less formal procedures and rules, fewer hierarchical levels – between the individual public servant and the overall policy goals. While smallness makes professionalization and formalization difficult, it can foster good administration through these other, non-Weberian ways.

At the macro level of the administrative system, a lack of specialization and professionalization implies a lack of bureaucratic autonomy. This lack, as Dahlström, Lapuente, and Teorell (2012) have shown, can be detrimental to administrative performance. Restricted by their small size, these bureaucracies and their bureaucrats have more difficulties in developing a distinct bureaucratic identity or "esprit de corps" (Rauch and Evans 2000, 52) than their larger counterparts and in gaining the usually theorized information advantages vis-à-vis politicians (Dumont and Varone 2006, 65–66). In their everyday work, they are more connected but may also be under more direct control by politicians. In small states, government politicians typically control most of the scarce resources, and public jobs are an important political resource. Powerful small state governments can easily capture the under-specialized national bureaucracies of small states (Dumont and Varone 2006, 63, 66; Veenendaal 2014, 157, 212), which may encourage forms of patronage and clientelism and hinder effective administrative practices (Dumont and Varone 2006, 67, 71; Sutton 1987, 15; Veenendaal and Corbett 2015, 539). On the other hand, smallness also restricts the capacities of governments and legislatures to exercise oversight over the administration (Corbett 2015, 62; Dumont and Varone 2006, 67; Sarapuu 2010, 36), which would increase administrators' room for maneuver.

It is important to note that administrative practices in small states are not simply a mirror image of practices in larger states. They are not defined exclusively by the lack of size, specialization, and Weberian features. Rather, the meta context of small states and societies produces additional characteristics that influence administrative practices: the role of proximity, personal ties, and informality (Corbett 2015; Jugl 2020b, 83; Sarapuu 2010). The small size of the administration and of single administrative organizations allows many bureaucrats to know each other personally and maintain personal relationships. In addition, small country size affects administrations through the size of the society and the resulting dense social relations: the key concept is again "polyvalence," but here, it is used to highlight the fact that individual public servants occupy several, overlapping roles in the private and professional realm. And, because the private realm is as restricted numerically as the realm of public administration, it is very likely that the same individuals interact in both worlds. Dense social networks with a prevalence of kin and personal ties permeate small societies and overlap with professional roles (Benedict 1967, 6–9; Lowenthal 1987, 30–33). Anthropologists Gingrich and Hannerz (2017, 18), for example, suggest that small units display "role combinations that might seem surprising to an observer from a country of another size," a situation "where the same people show up in many roles, knowing each other and perhaps knowing too much about each other." It is common in small states that public employees know their colleagues not only from collaboration at work but also through personal contacts, which qualify their work interactions. If a small state has only one university, it is most likely that top bureaucrats knew each other as students and share a similar educational experience. In theoretical terms, these features of small societies lead to more similar backgrounds (Dahl and Tufte 1973, 30–31) and more personalized relations and interactions within small state administrations. Several case studies have testified to the empirical importance of kin ties (e.g. Corbett 2015) and personal relations (Corbett and Veenendaal 2018; Veenendaal 2020) for small state politics, which is closely intertwined with public administration. Although empirical studies of these phenomena in public administration are largely lacking (but see Thorhallsson 2000 on personal relations), it is plausible to assume that they also dominate there.

The literature is quite clear, however, that this particular social environment promotes informal administrative practices (Dumont and Varone 2006, 53; Randma-Liiv and Sarapuu 2019, 165–66; Sarapuu 2010, 35–36): bureaucrats in small states often report that they simply pick up the phone and directly call their colleagues or politicians who are responsible for a certain topic, thus bypassing formal hierarchies. This common practice makes coordination within the public sector quicker and more flexible, but it blurs lines of responsibility and accountability. Proximity and personal relations can also plausibly enhance trust within and between administrative organizations, which can partly substitute formal monitoring institutions, reduce communication and administrative costs, and boost effectiveness (Bjørnskov 2010, 325–28, 344; Dumont and Varone 2006, 67, 71). This informal control could, however, be perverted and lead to a lack of effective monitoring or to the abovementioned capture and clientelism (Bräutigam and Woolcock 2001, 4).

Looking beyond the administrative system, the smallness of society and the limited number of public actors allow politicians and bureaucrats to be in close contact with each other and with citizens (Gingrich and Hannerz 2017, 28; Lowenthal 1987, 30). The lack of professionalism in the administration explained previously, together with the typical nearness of politicians and bureaucrats due to common educational backgrounds or personal relations, may encourage forms of nepotism or clientelism and hinder the effective fulfilling of administrative functions (Dumont and Varone 2006, 67, 71; Sutton 1987, 15; Veenendaal and Corbett 2015, 539). Moreover, informality also dominates public employees' interactions with citizens. Sutton (1987, 15) portrayed this in a very positive light: "senior administrative and political office holders have more direct contact with the man in the street, and accordingly there is less of the aloofness traditionally associated with a bureaucracy." Yet we should be careful in our analysis: if a bureaucrat personally knows a citizen requesting a public service, which is more likely in small societies, it becomes more difficult to follow formal, Weberian rules and ensure neutrality and impersonal treatment. Depending on whether close relations among bureaucrats and between bureaucrats and citizens are friendly or hostile, they might either increase levels of trust, facilitate and accelerate administrative procedures, or, on the contrary, block them and inhibit the professional functioning of the administration.

As we have seen, a certain size and degree of specialization are prerequisites for a formal, professional public administration. What exact size and degree of specialization remain an empirical question. It may be that the necessary country size is not gigantic, but rather medium level in a global comparison. The reader may think of examples of states with 10 or 30 million inhabitants that approximate Weber's ideal. At the same time, a medium size of country and administration may prevent the pathologies associated with extreme bureau-cratization and formalization and allow for some of the advantages of small-ness. In short, we can expect medium states to combine formal and informal administrative practices.

2.3 Size Effects on Performance

Finally, we can ask how country size affects how well public administra-tions function. How do size effects on structure and practice play out in terms of performance? It is helpful at this point to summarize the previous arguments:

- Large states can benefit from specialization at the macro, meso, and micro levels of public administration, which allows for professional and formalized practices and the realization of economies of scale. On the other hand, these benefits come with downsides, the diseconomies of scale including various bureaucratic pathologies and increased internal management costs.
- Small states struggle to realize economies of scale, are structurally inhibited in developing a professional rational-bureaucratic public administration, and are systematically at risk of patronage and clientelism. However, their administrative performance can benefit from informal coordination through personal ties and from motivation based on clearer identification with over-arching policy goals. This should minimize costs for internal administration and formal control mechanisms.
- Medium-sized states reach an intermediate level of structural specialization with only limited risks of bureaucratic pathologies while allowing for some degree of professionalization and a mix of formal and informal coordination practices.

Which aspects will prevail and determine overall public service performance? I expect that the downsides overshadow positive effects at the extremes of country size. I expect that moving on the country size continuum from an extremely small to a moderately small state will allow for modest specialization and economies of scale while maintaining the advantages of smallness. However, this should not be a simple monotonic relation (or "the larger, the better performing") because as country size increases, a tipping point will be reached after which diseconomies of scale will outweigh the advantages (Alesina and Spolaore 2005, 3–7; Tullock 1969, 25). I thus expect an inverse U-shaped relationship between a country's population size and national-level public service performance. Figure 2 illustrates this relation as a result of economies and diseconomies of scale. Scholars like Alesina and Spolaore (2005, 7) and Boyne (1995, 220) have theorized a curvilinear relationship between jurisdictional size and performance, but they have not tested it empirically at the national level. This inverse U should reach its peak at a medium country size. This point in the middle of the size continuum can be considered ideal if the aim is to maximize administrative performance. This is the "golden mean," where I expect a virtuous combination of "the best of both worlds." A medium size means a greater opportunity to combine a sufficient degree of the desired characteristics of the ideal-typical large and small bureaucracies (economies of scale and informal coordination), which are both expected to be necessary for reaching high levels of public service performance.

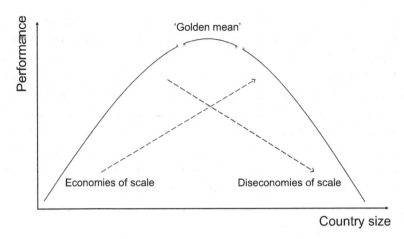

Figure 2 Theoretical model

To illustrate these arguments about the size-performance relationship, consider this quote about administrative impartiality, a central dimension of good administrative performance: "Weberian bureaucracy may in some areas be an incarnation of the impartiality principle but so may a public organization that is based on strong commitment to the policy goals while implementing these goals with a degree of flexibility" (Rothstein and Teorell 2008, 178). Rothstein and Teorell argue that Weberian structures and practices alone do not guarantee good and impartial administration but that a commitment to overarching policy goals is also important. In other words, the advantages of either big or small are not a silver bullet for reaching the highest levels of administrative performance. Both may lead to good results in specific cases but on average a combination, or the best of both worlds, should outperform them. In the present framework, medium-sized countries have the possibility to combine the advantages associated with large and small countries, and this gives them the potential to achieve the highest performance levels. Of course, all of these arguments are restricted by the ceteris paribus assumption. What exactly constitutes a medium-sized country is an empirical question that will be addressed in the following sections, together with extensive tests and illustrations of the theoretical framework.

3 Indicators and Correlations

Can we observe the theorized effects of size when considering more than single cases of small countries? This first empirical section presents several indicators that describe administrative systems across the world. It explores whether and how these features are related to country size. This approach builds on a descriptive quantitative comparison. Given the novelty of the comparative study of size effects on public administration, the aim is to map the varieties of public administration systems along the continuum of country size.

Table 1 provides an overview of the data sources and variables used. Following the theoretical framework, the measures are grouped into administrative structure, practices, and performance. The third column provides the correlation coefficient for each variable with population size. Population size data are from the Word Bank from 2018, while data for the administrative variables come from a range of years between 2016 and 2020. To illustrate the range of countries included in each correlation, the last two columns report the value of the respective measure for the smallest and largest countries included.

3.1 Structure

The strongest correlations are between country size and the size of the administrative system. According to data from the International Labor Organization (ILO 2021), total public employment in the public sector as a whole correlates at a spectacular 0.97 with population size. In short, this means that larger countries have larger public sectors in absolute terms, which reflects primarily the higher absolute demand for public services and is likely driven by more public employees in "street level" services, including in the police, health, and education systems.

However, a strong correlation with population size remains when we zoom in on public employment numbers solely at the central government level. Central government employment ranges from a mere 36,979 in Luxembourg (with a total population of about 0.6 million in 2018) to 4.17 million in the United States (with 327 million inhabitants). Although Luxembourg is a unitary and centralized state and the United States is a federal, decentralized system, their extreme difference in country size results in a much larger central government in the United States, in absolute numbers. Figure 3 illustrates the strong link between the size of the population and the size of the central government. In order to fit extremely large countries on the graph while also visualizing relative differences at small and medium levels of size, I employ a log scale of population size in this and the following scatterplots. The scale essentially compresses large values of size to fit very large countries like the United States in the graph. This way, the global median of country size, which is around 10 million in 2018, can be found at the center of these plots. The labels on the *x*-axis still indicate the population in millions. For reasons of readability, these plots feature only

Table 1 Correlation between population size and administrative features

DIMENSION Indicator (Source)	Countries (region) covered	Correlation with population size	Smallest country's value	Largest country's value
STRUCTURE				
Size of PA				
Public employment, total public sector (ILO 2021)	40	0.97**	Iceland: 50,466	USA: 24.59 mil
Public employment, central government (ILO 2021)	31	0.74**	Luxembourg: 36,979	USA: 4.17 mil
Vertical specialization				
Subnational institutional depth (Hooghe et al. 2021)	87	0.51**	Barbados: 0	China: 5.99
Employment share at central level (OECD 2019)	27 (OECD)	−0.24	Estonia: 48.5%	USA: 18.3%
Horizontal specialization				
Number of ministers (OECD 2019)	38 (OECD)	−0.02	Iceland: 9	USA: 15
PRACTICES				
Professionalism (Nistotskaya et al. 2020)	74	0.05	Iceland: 1.65	China: −0.15
Professionalism (MIF 2020)	51 (Africa)	−0.13	Seychelles: 50	Nigeria: 25
Interministerial coordination (SGI 2020)	41 (OECD & EU)	0.04	Iceland: 6	USA: 6.8

PERFORMANCE

Government Effectiveness (Kaufmann, Kraay, and Mastruzzi 2009)	168	0.06	Seychelles: 0.50	China: 0.48
Impartial public administration (Nistotskaya et al. 2020)	79	−0.18	Iceland: 1.44	China: −0.58
Citizen satisfaction with public service provision (European Commission 2019)	28 (EU)	−0.18	Malta: 75%	Germany: 74%
Public perception of public administration (MIF 2020)	34 (Africa)	−0.12	São Tomé and Príncipe: 68.8	Nigeria: 33.7

Note: For details on the sources and indicators, see text; **significant at $p < 0.5$

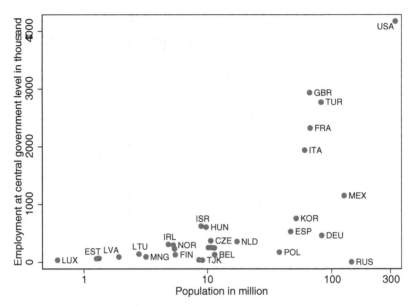

Figure 3 Total employment in central government (ILO) and population size

selected country labels, others are omitted to avoid overlaps. The empirical link
shown in Figure 3 supports the key assumption of the theoretical framework that
larger countries have larger administrations, beyond the "mechanical" increase
in teachers and police officers. However, the graph also shows some variation
among countries of comparable size, which points to differences in the degree
of centralization.

A fair share of decentralization and vertical specialization between levels of
governments can be linked to country size. I use two indicators to operation-
alize vertical specialization. The first is an indicator of "Institutional Depth" at
the subnational level based on expert assessments (Hooghe et al. 2021). It
captures the institutionalization and autonomy of each regional unit, from 0
(no administration at the regional level) to 1 (deconcentrated administrations,
i.e., regional offices of central government ministries under direct supervision
of central government), 2 (regional general-purpose administrations subject to
central government veto), and 3 (regional general-purpose administration that
is not deconcentrated and not subject to central government veto). The region-
specific scores are weighted by population and aggregated at the country level.
The final country score starts at zero and has no upper limit; it depends on the
number of tiers and the relative population weights of individual regions or
tiers. This indicator is available for more than 80 countries around the world
and correlates significantly at 0.51 with population size. The smallest countries covered here, including Barbados, Malta, Suriname, and Bhutan have

a score of zero with no functioning general-purpose administration at the regional level whatsoever. The largest countries without any regional-level administration are Jamaica, with just below 3 million inhabitants, and Singapore with roughly 5.5 million and the unique characteristics of a city-state. In contrast, the largest countries covered in the data set – Indonesia, the United States, India, and China – exhibit considerable degrees of vertical specialization with several regional administrative tiers. Regional administration in China, for example, includes the levels of greater administrative areas, prefectures, counties, provinces as well as autonomous regions, special economic zones, and special administrative regions (Hooghe et al. 2021).

The second indicator of vertical specialization is based again on employment numbers (OECD 2019): OECD statistics allow calculation of the share of government staff employed at the central level (compared to total government employment across all levels). The correlation coefficient is negative as expected, with larger states having a smaller share employed at the central level, but the correlation is not significant or large. The scatterplot in Figure 4 shows the considerable variation in centralization across countries. The relationship between size and public employment centralization is "diluted" by the European federations Belgium and Switzerland and by the Scandinavian countries, which are extremely decentralized despite having relatively small

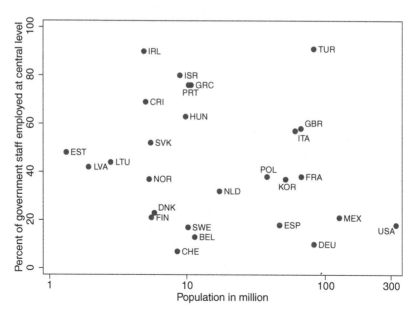

Figure 4 Share of government employment at central level (OECD) and population size

populations. Another deviating case is Turkey, a comparably large country but with a strong legacy of centralization (Hooghe et al. 2016, 511–12). This closer inspection suggests that national and regional traditions also play a considerable role besides size and functional pressures in determining the degree of vertical specialization.

To measure horizontal specialization within central governments, I use OECD data about the number of central government departments in 2019 (OECD 2019). In contrast to theoretical expectations, the number of departments does not increase systematically with country size; the correlation coefficient is close to zero. The data show large variations among small- and medium-sized countries. The smallest number of departments was recorded for Switzerland at 7 (for a population of roughly 8.5 million), whereas the maximum of 32 was registered in New Zealand (with just below 5 million inhabitants). At the other extreme, the 2 largest countries in the sample have modest numbers of government departments: 11 in Japan and 15 in the United States. These numbers allow for two conclusions. First, horizontal specialization, as measured through the number of central government departments, is not as linked with country size as vertical specialization (Gerring and Veenendaal 2020, 99; Thijs, Hammerschmid, and Palaric 2018, 17). Yet, a look beyond the OECD countries covered here shows that India with a population of more than 1.3 billion has around 40 ministries at the central government level, many of which comprise 2 or 3 government departments.[2] Government ministries are highly thematically specialized, for example, there is a Ministry for Textiles, a Ministry of Steel, a Ministry of Railways, and a Ministry of Tourism. This example is suggestive evidence for horizontal specialization being linked with large country size. Second, the number of central government departments may not perfectly capture the concept of functional specialization at the central government level. It may be, for example, that a modest number of government departments, as in the United States, hides a much larger number of specialized government agencies. In the case of Japan, 19 ministers head 11 government departments at the central level. In New Zealand, on the other hand, 32 government departments or portfolios were headed by only 19 ministers; their overlapping leadership roles bridge the institutional boundaries between ministries. These examples illustrate that comparative measurement of administrative units across countries is challenging.

---

[2] https://theprint.in/theprint-essential/youth-affairs-in-2000-to-cooperation-in-2021-heres-how-new-ministries-are-formed/691599/ and www.india.gov.in/my-government/whos-who/council-ministers (both accessed October 28, 2021).

3.2 Practices

Moving to the next part of the theoretical framework, administrative practices, I employ country-level indicators of professionalism and coordination in public administration. The Quality of Government Expert Survey (Nistotskaya et al. 2020) provides measures for administrative practices that are comparable across countries. The variable for professionalism is an index including the assessment of the role of patronage, merit, and job security in public employment by more than 550 experts. We do not observe any direct correlation between this index and country size. Large countries, including Indonesia, Brazil, the United States, China, and India, score in the middle of the professionalism scale, whereas there is extreme variation among smaller states. Among very small countries, Iceland reaches an upper-medium level of professionalism, and Albania and North Macedonia reach very low values. Notably, the highest values are reached by countries with a medium size between 4.9 million (Ireland and New Zealand) and 67 million (France and the United Kingdom). At the same time, the lowest level of professionalism is reported for Venezuela, which may have less to do with its medium size (around 29 million) than its political regime. Besides size, political and cultural factors seem to matter for public administration professionalism. Most likely, the levels of development and democracy, which are correlated with size (Corbett and Veenendaal 2018; Easterly and Kraay 2000), confound the hypothesized relation between size and professionalism. In this case, pure bivariate correlations (and scatterplots) overlook the underlying relation. Moreover, linear correlations may overlook curvilinear effects, for example, when medium size is linked with the highest degrees of professionalism.

Similar observations can be made for another measure of administrative professionalism. The variable "Professional Administration" from the Mo Ibrahim Foundation (MIF 2020) combines data from the African Development Bank, Global Integrity, and the World Bank. This continuous index covers all African countries and ranges from 0 to 100. This indicator has a modest negative correlation with size, suggesting that smaller countries have more professional administrations than larger ones. Figure 5 illustrates this weak empirical trend that would appear to run counter to theoretical expectations. The smallest country, Seychelles, reaches a score of 50, and the largest states Egypt and Nigeria, with populations of around 100 and 200 million, respectively, score considerably lower on professional administration with scores of 25. An explanation for this negative relation may be that small states need to hire relatively more highly educated bureaucrats to be able to cover high-level tasks, but because of polyvalence, they do more work that they are

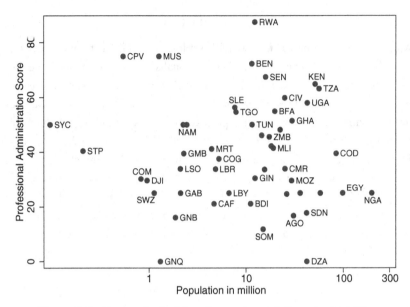

Figure 5 Professional administration and population size in Africa

overqualified for than their peers in larger countries. Again, the linear correlation analysis may hide a curvilinear relation: the highest-scoring country is medium-sized Rwanda with a population of around 12 million, which is not particularly rich or democratic compared to its African peers. Rwanda is an example of a medium-sized country that approximates Weber's ideal of a professional bureaucracy with a strong and capable "developmental state" (Mann and Berry 2016) that focuses on performance and fostering growth.

The final indicator of public administration practices measures interministerial coordination in OECD and EU countries (SGI 2020). Constructed by the Bertelsmann Foundation's Sustainable Governance Indicators Project and based on country experts' assessment of several questions, the indicator captures how well government decision making is coordinated across institutional lines, including formal and informal practices to coordinate policy formulation and decision making across government ministries and with the central government office. The correlation coefficient between interministerial coordination and population size is close to zero. Finland, with a population of around 5.5 million, had the highest score in 2019; this is based on a fruitful combination of formal and informal meetings to coordinate large-scale policies and detailed policy proposals and on smooth collaboration between cabinet ministers and senior civil servants (SGI 2020). Cyprus, with 1.2 million inhabitants, received the lowest coordination score. In practice, coordination is limited in small Cyprus because the Council of Ministers lacks administrative resources and practices to evaluate and comprehensively coordinate proposals from line ministries; informal meetings are used infrequently (SGI 2020). A closer inspection reveals that these examples are indicative of a geographic pattern with countries from Southern and Eastern Europe scoring lower on coordination and countries from Northern and Western Europe (plus other OECD countries like New Zealand, Canada, and South Korea) scoring higher. This geographic pattern points to the role of administrative traditions and legacies (Kuhlmann and Wollmann 2014).

3.3 Performance

Ultimately, we are interested in the relationship between country size and administrative performance. I use four indicators of public service performance to illuminate this relation, beginning with the variable "Government Effectiveness" from the World Bank's Worldwide Governance Indicators (WGI; Kaufmann, Kraay, and Mastruzzi 2009). The indicator combines several data sources on perceptions of the quality and effectiveness of public services, the civil service, policy formulation, and implementation. The data come from surveys, nongovernmental organizations, commercial information providers, and country assessments by international organizations. They are based on the judgment of external stakeholders (citizens, entrepreneurs, and mostly experts), who are usually less suspected of systematically overreporting performance than stakeholders inside the bureaucracy. The reliance on subjective measures may still involve some reliability issues (Walker, Boyne, and Brewer 2010, 11–14), which have been widely discussed for the WGI (Langbein and Knack 2010; Kurtz and Schrank 2007; van de Walle 2006). However, the WGI's combination and triangulation of diverse data sources through an unobserved components model ensures the representativeness of the respondents' judgments, minimizes the effect of individual respondents' biases, and allows for a broad country coverage. These are the main reasons why the WGI remain a widely used cross-country measure for public service performance. Broad data availability allows us to calculate the correlation between the WGI's Government Effectiveness variable and population size for 168 countries in 2018. The correlation coefficient is close to zero, suggesting no direct relationship between the two. Figure 6 illustrates this for a global and highly diverse sample of countries. The smallest and largest countries in the sample, Seychelles and China, have almost identical scores on this variable of close to 0.5. The highest values are reached, again, by medium-sized countries close to the global median of around 10 million inhabitants. With populations of between 5 and 9 million, Finland, Singapore and Switzerland

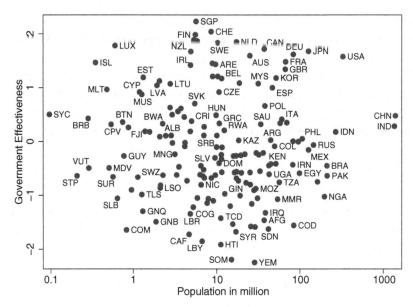

Figure 6 Government Effectiveness (WGI) and population size

appear to combine the best of both worlds (large and small), with their scores being more than 2 standard deviations above the mean Government Effectiveness. For the sake of completeness, it bears mentioning that the lowest scores are held by Libya, Haiti, Somalia, and Yemen, countries that are neither particularly small nor large but that are challenged by internal conflicts and war. As with previous indicators, Government Effectiveness seems to be linked not only with size but also with geographic, cultural, and political aspects.

Another important dimension of administrative performance is administrative impartiality, which I have mentioned in Section 2. The Quality of Government Expert Survey (Nistotskaya et al. 2020; see previous discussion) measures impartiality as the degree to which bureaucrats, when implementing laws or regulations, take no information or circumstances about a person or case into account other than those required by the law. This expert-coded variable correlates only weakly and negatively with population size. The smallest country covered is democratic Iceland with an impartiality score of 1.44, and the largest is communist China where the more politicized administration reaches a negative impartiality score of –0.58. The most impartial administration is that of Finland (1.63). Finland's population is about 16 times larger than Iceland's but 252 times smaller than that of China.

The final two indicators enable us to zoom in on more homogenous groups of countries and to observe perceptions of public service users or citizens. For the EU-28 countries, the Eurobarometer survey (European Commission 2019) asks citizens about their satisfaction with how public services are provided in their country. The percentage of satisfied citizens correlates slightly negatively with population size. Although the smallest and largest EU member states, Malta and Germany, reach similar satisfaction levels (75 percent and 74 percent, respectively), there is a pattern with smaller and medium-sized EU states reaching higher levels of citizen satisfaction on average than their larger peers. In EU studies, the traditional cutoff for small states – or states that are "not large" – has been the size of the Netherlands (Neumann and Gstöhl 2006, 6), which currently has a population of around 17 million. Note that in international comparison, this is not particularly small but midsize. In small and midsize EU states up to the Netherlands, 61 percent of citizens are satisfied on average with public service provision (taking the simple average of country values), compared to an average of 49 percent in the seven larger states. However, a difference-of-means test (t-test, not shown here) indicates that this difference is not statistically significant. Size alone cannot account for this variation in performance. Rather, low levels of citizen satisfaction are clustered in Southern, Eastern, and English-speaking member states, groups that include all of the larger countries (France, Italy, Spain, Poland, Romania, and the United Kingdom) except for Germany.

A related measure, "Public perception of public administration," is available from the Mo Ibrahim Foundation for several African countries (MIF 2020). This indicator, ranging from 0 to 100, is based on 2 items from the Afrobarometer survey that capture citizen satisfaction with the ease of obtaining an identity document and essential services. Like satisfaction in EU states, this indicator of satisfaction with public administration in 34 African countries has a weak negative correlation with population size. The smallest state covered is São Tomé and Príncipe with a population of around 200,000 and a satisfaction score of 69.8, and the largest state, Nigeria, reaches a score of 33.7. Public perceptions of the quality of public administration are highest in Botswana, with just above 2 million inhabitants and a score of 82.3. Indeed, Botswana and Nigeria are influential cases that drive the weak negative association. The main takeaway from citizen satisfaction in EU and African states is that it tends to be lower in large countries.

What can we conclude from the analysis of indicators and their correlations with size? The variety of sources and indicators allows for an overview of size and public administration across the globe. We have seen that population size is systematically linked with the absolute size of an administrative system and with the size of central government employment. There is also a clear link between size and the level of vertical specialization through decentralization.

Horizontal specialization, as measured by the number of government departments, does not appear to be systematically related to size. This operationalization is far from ideal, though, especially given the trend of agencification in the past decades. In this sense, the null finding for government ministries does not suffice to disconfirm the theoretical predictions of greater specialization within central governments. Indicators of administrative practices and performance do not correlate linearly with country size. Instead, best-rated practices are found in midsize countries, and performance indicators are particularly low in large states. Importantly, there is high variation in the level of professionalism, coordination, impartiality, and citizen satisfaction, especially among small- and medium-sized countries. Bivariate, linear correlations are insufficient for exploring size effects for two main reasons. First, the inspection of country scores and scatterplots has uncovered clustering in terms of geographic, cultural, and political factors. Bivariate correlations cannot account or control for these additional factors and their effect on administrative practices and performance. Second, the highest values on several indicators were reached by midsize countries, including Rwanda among the African countries, Finland among the OECD countries, and Singapore in a global comparison. These findings may suggest a curvilinear relationship between size on the one hand and professionalism, coordination, and performance on the other. This is in line with the theoretical arguments developed earlier that medium size, from a global or regional perspective, can allow for sufficient specialization and professionalism while limiting the risk of bureaucratic pathologies. These findings offer preliminary support to the idea that good features of small and large size can complement each other at a *golden mean*, in a midsize country with favorable political and economic circumstances. To explore the curvilinear relation further and move beyond the methodological limitations of descriptive, bivariate analyses, the next section introduces more sophisticated statistical techniques.

4 Causal Statistical Analysis

The aim of this empirical section is to test the hypothesized inverse U-shaped relationship between country size and public service performance with a global, cross-country statistical analysis.[3] The section focuses on the last link in the theoretical framework: the relationship between size and performance. Can we uncover a systematic link between the two when going beyond the simple correlations examined in the previous section?

---

[3] The analysis in this section is adopted from Jugl (2019).

To measure performance, I employ the WGI's "Government Effectiveness" indicator mentioned in the previous section. As shown in Table 1, this indicator has a very extensive country coverage making it "the most comprehensive dataset" (van de Walle 2006, 440) of its kind, which is essential for studying the effect of state size in its breadth. The reason for this broad coverage lies in the aggregation method, in which several items from the underlying sources are integrated in slightly varying combinations, into one standardized score for each country-year. By allowing data sources to differ between countries and years, the measure reaches high coverage of countries and years and lends itself to temporal and between-country comparisons (Kaufmann, Kraay, and Mastruzzi 2009). The indicator is available biannually from 1996 to 2000 and annually since 2002. The analyses in this section utilize data up to 2014, based on the WGI version updated in 2015.

The other central variable, the independent variable of interest, is population size. This measure is easily available from the World Bank for virtually all countries in the world and annually for the period of study. However, as we have seen in the previous section, population size is an extremely skewed variable in global comparison, as well as in single continents and world regions. The standard remedy for such skewness is to log-transform the variable. Essentially, this transformation keeps the order of the observations (countries) but compresses large values. Figure 7 illustrates how the distribution changes through log transformation. Next, I introduce three statistical modeling strategies to estimate the effect of (log) population size on Government Effectiveness. I discuss the logic behind each approach and their respective results in turn.

4.1 Cross-sectional Models

To move beyond linear correlations, I model the expected inverse U-shaped relationship with population size (log-transformed) and its quadratic term as key explanatory variables. The first part of the analysis utilizes a simple cross-sectional model with data for 2014 (see Jugl 2019 for various other years). Since the explanatory variable of interest (population size) and the dependent variable (Government Effectiveness) are continuous, ordinary least squares (OLS) estimation is appropriate. The basic regression model is:

$$GE_j = \beta_0 + \beta_1 LPOP_j + \beta_2 LPOP_j^2 + \gamma_3 C_j + e_j, \tag{1}$$

where GE_j is Government Effectiveness in country j, $LPOP_j$ is the natural logarithm of the country's population size and $LPOP_j^2$ is its square, C_j is a vector of controls, and e_j is the error term. The coefficients of top priority are

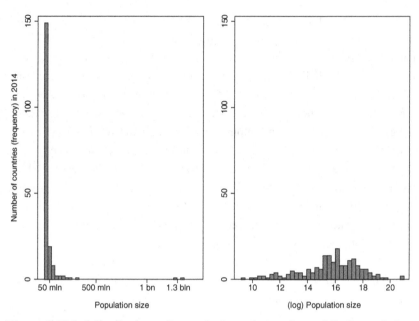

Figure 7 Global distributions of countries' population size and (log) population size in 2014

β_1 and β_2, and they are expected to be larger than zero (β_1) and smaller than zero (β_2), respectively, to model an inverse U-shaped relationship.

The bivariate analyses in the previous section identified economic and political factors as potential determinants of administrative performance. Therefore, the baseline model includes two control variables. The first is economic development (GDP per capita, logged) because high-income countries tend to achieve higher levels of public service performance (Rauch and Evans 2000, 57). The second is political regime type (Freedom House) because democracy is related to high levels of performance (Bäck and Hadenius 2008). I use the indicator "Political rights" from Freedom House because of its extensive country coverage, including very small states, but I invert the scale so that high values mean high levels of freedom and democracy.

Previous studies on the determinants of public service performance inform the choice of further control variables. These include dummy variables for legal origin following La Porta and colleagues (1999) as a proxy for administrative and state traditions. This data source has wide country coverage and classifies the legal origin of a country's commercial code as one out of five options: British, Socialist, French, German, and Scandinavian. These categories overlap with specific welfare regimes and capture historical patterns of the role of the state and of preferences for a "bigger" or "leaner" state. It has been widely argued that the institutions originating from a British legacy are conducive to high public service performance. Moreover, I use the share of the urban population (World Bank) and education levels as controls for the level of societal development and as a proxy for knowledgeable citizens who are expected to be more critical of bureaucratic inefficiencies. I measure education by the expected average years of schooling (CIA 2021) because this is the only available measure with extensive country coverage. I also test further controls: population growth based on yearly population data to distinguish analytically between the effects of population stocks (size) and flows (growth); ethnic fractionalization (Alesina et al. 2003), which is expected to negatively influence public service performance because it increases the complexity of bureaucracy and society (Alesina, Baqir, and Easterly 1999; Habyarimana et al. 2007); and a dummy for federal states (Norris 2009) that is expected to attenuate diseconomies of scale in large states. For details on all data sources and descriptive statistics, see Jugl (2019, appendix).

Table 2 reports results from these cross-sectional models. Model 1 is the baseline model with economic development and regime type as control variables, which both have the expected positive effect here and in all following models. The coefficients for (log) population size and its squared term are significant and show the expected signs. The two baseline controls are sufficient to uncover a systematic, curvilinear size effect on performance data that are similar to those shown in Figure 6. Model 2 adds two control variables, share of urban population and education, which increase the explanatory power of the model but the controls themselves have no significant effect. This specification also adds dummy variables for legal origin as proxies for administrative traditions. Model 2 is the best fitting cross-sectional model with regard to the control variables; it explains about 81 percent of global variation (R^2) in Government Effectiveness. The introduction of further controls for ethnic fractionalization, population growth, and federalism in Model 3 does not increase the explanatory power of the model but further reduces the country coverage due to data limitations. Therefore, I use the control variables from Model 2 in all the following models.

Model 4 reports regression results for the subsample of democratic countries with controls as before. Thus, it zooms in on a smaller subsample of countries with more homogenous political conditions. A country is defined as a democracy if it has a score of 5.5 or higher on Freedom House's inversed political rights scale, which is in accordance with Freedom House's coding rules. The coefficients for (log) population size and its squared term for democracies are highly significant and show the expected signs. The fit of the cross-sectional model is even higher for democracies than for the global sample; it

Table 2 Regression results from cross-sectional models for 2014

	Global sample			Democracies only
	(1)	(2)	(3)	(4)
(log) population	0.500**	0.573*	0.547*	0.837**
	(0.162)	(0.236)	(0.251)	(0.262)
[(log) population]^2	−0.014*	−0.016*	−0.015$^+$	−0.024**
	(0.005)	(0.007)	(0.008)	(0.008)
(log) GDP pc	0.482**	0.424**	0.448**	0.478**
	(0.030)	(0.064)	(0.068)	(0.072)
Political rights	0.129**	0.118**	0.118**	0.266*
	(0.023)	(0.024)	(0.028)	(0.112)
Urbanization		−0.004	−0.005	−0.006
		(0.003)	(0.004)	(0.004)
Exp. school years		0.034	0.024	0.027
		(0.026)	(0.026)	(0.031)
Fractionalization			0.051	–
			(0.188)	
Population growth			0.002	–
			(0.040)	

	(1)	(2)	(3)	(4)
Federalism			−0.104	—
			(0.130)	
Legal origin dummies	No	Yes	Yes	Yes
Constant	−9.21**	−9.36**	−9.29**	−12.64**
	(1.23)	(1.93)	(2.02)	(2.16)
Observations	176	162	159	74
Model fit	$R^2 = 0.77$	$R^2 = 0.81$	$R^2 = 0.81$	$R^2 = 0.86$
	$F = 141.7$**	$F = 110.2$**	$F = 87.6$**	$F = 53.7$**
Turning point	81 m	61 m	94 m	29 m

Note: Dependent variable is Government Effectiveness; standard errors in parentheses; OLS estimates with robust standard errors; turning point in million population; $^+ p < 0.1$, $* p < 0.05$, and $** p < 0.01$

explains about 86 percent of the variation in Government Effectiveness. According to the cross sectional model for democracies, an increase of the logarithm of population at low levels from 14 (or 1.2 m inhabitants) to 16 (8.9 m inhabitants) has a predicted effect of $(0.837 * 16 - 0.024 * 16^2) - (0.837 * 14 - 0.024 * 14^2) = 0.21$ on Government Effectiveness or an increase of about one-fifth of a standard deviation (since Government Effectiveness is standardized). At larger sizes, in contrast, an increase of the logarithm of population size from 18 (66 m inhabitants) to 20 (485 m inhabitants) is associated with a decrease in effectiveness by just under a fifth of a standard deviation (–0.18). Note that the logarithm hides that the positive effect at lower levels of size is steeper (an increase of only 7.7 m in size being associated with a performance increase of 0.21) than the negative effect at high levels (a 419 m increase leading to a 0.18 performance decrease).

4.2 Within-Between Random-Effects Models

The second modeling strategy is chosen to match the characteristics of the available data. I aim to analyze the data in a longitudinal format for the period 1996 through 2014, but at the same time, I focus on the theoretically relevant between-country effect. The hypothesized size effect on public service perform-ance applies to the difference between states of different sizes but not to changes within a country over time. For the period covered in this study, differences in population size are much larger between countries than within a country: simply put, a small country remains a small country. The results in Table 2 show that population growth, a measure of within-country change, has no significant nor substantial effect on performance. Likewise, administrative performance has been assumed as being relatively stable across years, decades, or even longer (Rauch and Evans 2000, 62). Because both key concepts are sticky over time, I expect no short-term within-country effects but focus instead on between-country effects.

Consequently, common fixed-effects (FE) models that control completely for between-country variation are not suitable. Country fixed effects would simply absorb the differences in population levels between countries. Meanwhile, a standard random-effects (RE) model is not appropriate either. An RE model calculates only one coefficient for each independent variable as a weighted mean of its between- and within-country effect and would "assume that the within- and between-country effects are equal" (Bartels 2008, 9; see also Snijders and Bosker 1999, 30). This would not be in line with the theoretical framework and expect-ations. Because of the limitations of these standard approaches, I utilize a multilevel "within-between RE model (REWB)" (Bell and Jones 2015, 145; see also Bartels 2008; Snijders and Bosker 1999, 27–29). REWB allows modeling and interpretation of within-country and between-country effects explicitly and separately within one model. Showing "the full picture" and allowing a comparison of effects make this technique superior to pure between-effect models that do not report the within-country effect. The REWB model builds on a temporal hierarchy, in which country-year observations (level 1) are nested within countries (level 2). It combines a level-1 equation, estimating the time-variant within-country effects, and a level-2 equation, explicitly modeling the time-invariant country effect. This reduces unobserved heterogeneity and corrects standard errors for country-level heterogeneity (Bell and Jones 2015, 142). What is crucial with regard to population size (and other time-variant variables) is that it enters the model twice: at the country level (level 2), the country mean for population size is used; at the country-year level (level 1), the yearly deviation from this country-specific mean is used (Bartels 2008, 11–12). The two-level model is thus:

$$GE_{ij} = \beta_0 + \beta_1 \overline{LPOP_j} + \beta_2 \overline{LPOP_j}^2 + \beta_3 \left(LPOP_{ij} - \overline{LPOP_j}\right)$$
$$+ \beta_4 \left(LPOP_{ij}^2 - \overline{LPOP_j}^2\right) + \beta_5 \overline{logGDPpc_j} + \beta_6 \left(logGDPpc_{ij}\right.$$
$$\left. - \overline{logGDPpc_j}\right) + \beta_6 \overline{POL_{RIGHTSj}} + \beta_7 \left(POL_{RIGHTSij}\right.$$
$$\left. - \overline{POL_{RIGHTSj}}\right) + u_j + e_{ij}, \tag{2}$$

where GE_{ij} is Government Effectiveness in year i and country j, $LPOP_{ij}$ is the natural logarithm of the country's population size in year i ($LPOP_{ij}^2$ is its square), $\overline{LPOP_j}$ is the mean of population size over the time of the study in country j ($\overline{LPOP_j}^2$ is its square), and u_j is the random effect for country j and e_{ij} is the country-year-specific error. The coefficients for the between-country effect of population size and squared population are β_1 and β_2; I expect them to be positive and negative, respectively. There are no clear expectations about the within-effect coefficients β_3 and β_4. For reasons of space and readability, the above formula includes only two control variables; more will be added with time-invariant variables (legal origin and education for lack of longitudinal data) entering the model only at the country level (level 2) and time-variant variables (GDP per capita, regime type, and share of urban population) included at both levels. The model is estimated by maximum likelihood (Bartels 2008, 15; Snijders and Bosker 1999, 56).

Table 3 reports the results of two multilevel REWB models based on data for 1996 through 2014. First, the within effects and between effects are reported for a global sample, and then the final two columns show the within and between effects for the subsample of democracies. The coefficients for the between effect of (log) population size and [(log) population size]^2 are significant and show the expected signs for an inverse U-shaped relation.

Table 3 Results from REWB models

	Global sample		Democracies only	
	(Within)	(Between)	(Within)	(Between)
(log) population	0.017	0.447*	1.092[+]	0.623**
	(0.351)	(0.176)	(0.604)	(0.178)
[(log) population]^2	−0.011	−0.012*	−0.058**	−0.018**
	(0.011)	(0.006)	(0.020)	(0.006)
(log) GDP pc	0.107**	0.423**	0.113**	0.~29**
	(0.011)	(0.041)	(0.017)	(0.046)
Political rights	0.031**	0.143**	0.097**	0.254**
	(0.006)	(0.018)	(0.024)	(0.052)
Urbanization	−0.007**	−0.005*	−0.009**	−0.005*
	(0.002)	(0.002)	(0.003)	(0.002)
Exp. school years		0.019		0.036
		(0.018)		(0.024)
Legal origin dummies		Yes		Yes
Random part				
Level-1 error, $\hat{\sigma}_e$	0.193 (0.003)		0.174 (0.004)	
Level-2 error, $\hat{\sigma}_u$	0.374 (0.021)		0.296 (0.023)	

Constant	−7.89**	−10.18**
	(1.41)	(1.39)
Observations	$N = 170$, total obs. = 2,669	$N = 92$, total obs. = 1,187
Model fit	Model $\chi^2 = 433.2$**	Model $\chi^2 = 286.5$**
Turning point	66 m	29 m

Note: Dependent variable is Government Effectiveness; standard errors in parentheses; REWB models with random intercept at the country level estimated via MLE; turning point in millions (population); $^+ p < 0.1$, $*p < 0.05$, and $** p < 0.01$

However, there is no clear within-country effect of population size; yearly population changes within a country have no systematic effects on administrative performance. The difference between within- and between-effects affirms the use of the REWB model compared to standard FE and RE approaches and illustrates its usefulness for dealing with sluggish variables. In contrast, the control variables GDP per capita, political rights, and urban population show significant within- and between-country effects with the same signs. The control variables exert significant influence in the expected direction, except for the share of urban population that has a constantly negative effect and education that remains insignificant.

The predictive margins in Figure 8 illustrate the curves resulting from the REWB model's between-country effect for the global sample and the democratic subsample with 95 percent confidence intervals. Initially, the predicted level of Government Effectiveness increases with size up to a turning point after which it decreases. The confidence intervals are inflated at higher levels of population size simply because there are few observations (countries) in this area as shown in Figure 7. Note that in all cross-sectional and REWB models and in Figure 8, the estimated effect size is moderate; substantial differences in population size have a significant but moderate impact on public service performance.

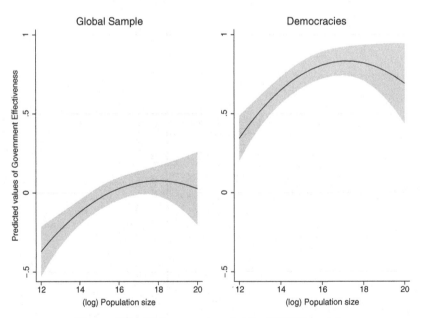

Figure 8 Predictive margins plot for REWB models
Note: Graphs based on REWB between effects (Table 3) with 95 percent confidence intervals.

4.3 Instrumental Variable Estimation

A potential threat to causal inference is endogeneity (for the endogeneity of contextual factors, see Ongaro, Gong, and Jing 2021, 7). For example, one may argue that there is reverse causality running from public service performance to population size. A well-performing public sector could, for example, encourage people to have more children, or it might attract immigrants, which both increase population size in the long run. A standard statistical approach to correct for potential endogeneity of this kind is instrumental variable (IV) estimation where a third, completely exogenous variable is used as an instrument.

Such an instrumental variable is often challenging to find. I follow the lead of political scientists and economists (Gerring, Jaeger, and Maguire 2016; Rose 2006) who have used (log) area as an exogenous instrument for (log) population size. It cannot be ruled out completely that area has an independent effect on performance, but it is very unlikely. A country's geographical size and the resulting internal distances were certainly a constraint on effective public service in historical eras when transport and communication were slow (Gerring, Jaeger, and Maguire 2016, 92). In the modern time period covered in this study with modern means of transport and communication, however, area seems to be less influential and exercises its main effect on performance via population size with which it is strongly correlated ($r = 0.85$ in 2014). Based on this assumption, I use (log) area and $[(\log)$ area$]^2$ as instruments for (log) population size and its squared term.

Table 4 reports detailed results and test statistics of both stages of the two-stage-least-squares estimation with the same controls as before, first for the global sample and then only for democracies. A Hausman test fails to reject the null hypothesis that the population size variables are exogenous for democracies, so the original OLS estimates in Table 2 can be regarded as sufficiently unbiased. For the global sample, however, the test rejects exogeneity and supports the use of instrumental variables. Accordingly, Table 4 reports also the second-stage results. For both samples, the results confirm the inverse U-shaped effect found in previous models, and the explanatory power of the models remains high.

With regard to the IV approach, it should be borne in mind that its interpretation and reliability depend on the exogeneity assumption for area, and it is left to the reader to judge its plausibility. In any case, the threat of reverse causality is limited in our empirical context: while public service performance can arguably influence population growth, this would change absolute population size only marginally in global comparison and over the long term rather than the short term. The size of all countries' populations in 2014 were remarkably

Table 4 Instrumental variable estimation (two-stage least squares)

	Global sample	Democracies
	First-stage regression	
(log) population size		
Correlation with (log) area	0.855**	0.880**
Partial r^2	0.674	0.650
Shea's partial r^2	0.499	0.481
F	156.00	140.25
[(log) population size]^2		
Correlation with [(log) area]^2	0.834**	0.862**
Partial r^2	0.664	0.637
Shea's partial r^2	0.483	0.464
F	62.13	55.35
	Second-stage regression	
(log) population size (instrumented)	0.885**	1.057**
	(0.292)	(0.317)
[(log) population size]^2 (instrumented)	−0.027**	−0.0032**
	(0.009)	(0.010)
(log) GDP pc	0.416**	0.464**
	(0.046)	(0.059)
Political rights	0.113**	0.245*
	(0.021)	(0.101)
Urbanization	−0.004	−0.006[+]
	(0.003)	(0.003)

Expected school years	0.036[+]	(0.020)	0.034	(0.029)
Legal origin dummies	Yes		Yes	
Constant	−11.41**	(2.27)	−13.99**	(2.36)
Observations	162		74	
Model fit	$R^2 = 0.80$		$R^2 = 0.85$	
Turning point	12 m		13 m	
Wu-Hausman, χ^2 and p (H_0: variables are exogenous)	8.01	$p = 0.018$	2.38	$p = 0.304$

Notes: Dependent variable is Government Effectiveness in 2014; standard errors for second stage in parentheses; turning point in millions (population);
[+] $p < 0.1$, * $p < 0.05$, and ** $p < 0.01$

highly correlated ($r = 0.99$) with their population sizes three decades before (1984). This shows that population size is extremely sluggish and above all driven by past levels of population size.

4.4 Interpretations

The use of cross-sectional and REWB models in this section proved appropriate because both isolate the theoretically relevant between-country effect of size. The IV approach demonstrated the robustness of the results and strengthened their causal interpretation. Taken together, the cross-sectional models in Table 2, the REWB models in Table 3 and Figure 8, and the IV results in Table 4 provide robust[4] evidence for the existence of economies of scale: a positive and steep effect of size on performance at lower levels of country size. These results fill an empirical gap that earlier conceptual contributions in the field of small-state studies had left open (Alesina and Spolaore 2005; Randma-Liiv 2002). The findings support the idea that small country size limits effectiveness and make clear that size matters specifically *among* non-large states: very small countries such as Monaco or Tuvalu are substantially different from small- or medium-sized countries such as Ireland or Tunisia that benefit already from economies of scale. The squared population size is also consistently significant, but the broad confidence intervals illustrated in Figure 8 lead us to question whether there is a downward slope at higher levels of population size or saturation with the upward slope simply stopped but not inversed. In either case, diseconomies of scale are evident and clearly stop the positive size effect of economies of scale after the optimal size is reached.

Tables 2–4 also report the turning points of the size effect as the empirical estimation of the optimal country size. They calculate the "golden mean" for administrative performance. I calculate the turning points from the coefficients on (log) population size and [(log) population size]^2 in the cross-sectional models (Tables 2 and 4) or, in the case of the multilevel model (Table 3), from their between-effect coefficients. The estimated turning points support the theoretical expectation that the maximum public service performance is found at medium population size. The turning points vary between models and samples used, from 12 m to 94 m, but they do not vary randomly: they tend to be lower when only democracies are considered. It could be argued that in democracies, which show, according to the data used here, higher average Government Effectiveness and which are smaller on average (Congdon Fors 2014; Diamond and Tsalik 1999), economies of scale are reached at a comparatively small size, and diseconomies of large size come into play more quickly than in less

---

[4] For various robustness checks, see Jugl (2019).

effective bureaucracies. The finding that medium country size is optimal for public service effectiveness fills an empirical gap and shows that negative effects of smallness are dominant up to medium population size. This finding was only possible by expanding the sample and variance in population size compared to previous studies, which assumed, for a lack of variation in country size, that the observed processes apply only to very small countries (Corbett, Veenendaal, and Connell 2021; Dumont and Varone 2006; Randma-Liiv and Sarapuu 2019).

The findings also point to the important role of political institutions and regime types. The curvilinear size effect is substantially larger for the democratic subsample than for the global sample. Democracies drive the effect in the global sample, whereas the effect does not appear among nondemocratic countries (not shown here). This indicates that the theorized mechanisms, derived mainly from literature on advanced democracies, work best in democratic countries. Democracies share the goal of high public service performance almost by design. Aiming for reelection, democratic politicians must be responsive and responsible to their citizens for the goods and services provided through the bureaucracy. This "democracy advantage" based on "three core characteristics of representative government: shared power, openness, and self-correcting capacity" (Halperin, Siegle, and Weinstein 2010, 13) is also reflected in the higher level of Government Effectiveness for democracies on average, regardless of country size (see Figure 8 and coefficients for political rights in all models). Nondemocratic countries, in contrast, are a much more heterogeneous group with regard to institutional arrangements and incentives for public service performance and thus more difficult to compare. The advanced statistical tools in this section allow us to disentangle these effects from the role of country size.

5 Comparative Cases: Germany, Luxembourg, and the Netherlands

5.1 Case Selection, Data, and Methods

This section uses a qualitative comparison and zooms in on three cases: Luxembourg, the Netherlands, and Germany. To identify and analyze the effects of country size, the case selection is based on a "most similar systems design" (Przeworski and Teune 1970; Slater and Ziblatt 2013). This research design starts from a theory-driven case selection that holds alternative explanatory factors constant in order to isolate the causal effect of interest. Luxembourg, the Netherlands, and Germany share many social, political, and economic characteristics, but they differ considerably in terms of population size. Table 5

Table 5 Country profiles and comparative setting

	Luxembourg	The Netherlands	Germany	Case congruence
GDP per capita, current USD	115,874	52,304	45,724	Moderately similar
EU membership	Founding member	Founding member	Founding member	Most similar
Political system	Liberal democracy	Liberal democracy	Liberal democracy	Most similar
Government system	Parliamentary with coalition governments	Parliamentary with coalition governments	Parliamentary with coalition governments	Most similar
Administrative tradition	Germanic and Napoleonic	Germanic with Scandinavian and Anglo-Saxon elements	Germanic	Sufficiently similar
Population size	0.6 million	17.4 million	83.2 million	Difference

Sources: CIA World Factbook accessed November 1, 2021 under www.cia.gov/the-world-factbook/countries/; data on population and GDP are from the World Bank for 2020 accessed November 1, 2021 under https://data.worldbank.org/, for administrative traditions see text.

summarizes the country profiles and important contextual factors for public administration.

The three countries are neighbors in continental Europe, and all three were founding members of the European Union's predecessor, the European Economic Community, in 1957. All three are wealthy, advanced economies. GDP per capita is relatively similar in Germany and the Netherlands but considerably higher in Luxembourg. This difference challenges the "most similar systems" approach. However, if anything, this gap should work against the hypothesized size effects because higher per capita income may ease some of the structural limitations of small size. If we still find evidence of resource scarcity in Luxembourg's public administration, despite higher GDP per capita, then this would strengthen the conclusions about a limiting effect of smallness. Luxembourg and the Netherlands are constitutional monarchies, while the German head of state is a president, yet in substantive terms, all three are stable liberal democracies with a parliamentary system. They share the practice of coalition government.

In terms of administrative and legal traditions, the three countries are also sufficiently similar. All three build on a Continental European *Rechtstaat* tradition based on a civil law system. In the comparative public administration literature, Germany is typically presented as a prototype of the Germanic, central European type (Kickert 2011; Kuhlmann and Wollmann 2014; Painter and Peters 2010). Although often mentioned in the same breath as Austria and Switzerland, Germany's larger size affords it a prominent position as the prototypical country. In stark contrast, the comparative literature largely ignores Luxembourg and does not assign it to a specific administrative tradition. When it is mentioned, Luxembourg has been labeled a continental European administration influenced by Germanic and Napoleonic legacies (Demmke and Moilanen 2010, 150; Ziller 2007, 167). The Netherlands is often considered a mixed case or not classified coherently (Pollitt and Bouckaert 2017, 62, 74; van der Meer 2018, 762). Kickert (2011) characterizes the Netherlands explicitly as a "Small Continental European State," while Painter and Peters (2010, 22) classify the country under the Germanic tradition. Pollitt and Bouckaert (2017, 62, 74) argue that the Netherlands moved away from a highly legalistic *Rechtsstaat* tradition and closer to the Scandinavian and Anglo-Saxon models. What is important for the comparative design of this section is that all three countries build to a considerable degree on a Continental–Germanic administrative tradition.

To analyze the effects of country size, the qualitative comparisons combine between-case comparison and thorough within-case analyses (Slater and Ziblatt 2013). Table 5 summarizes the degree of similarity between the three countries. Because these alternative explanations for administrative practices and performance are largely held constant by virtue of case selection, the resulting differences in the public administration systems can arguably be ascribed to differences in country size. The table shows that population size differs considerably. The Netherlands is 28.5 times larger than Luxembourg but almost 5 times smaller than Germany. Although the Netherlands is regularly referred to as the largest among the small EU countries (see discussion in Section 3.3), these population numbers show that its relative size gap with Luxembourg is larger than that with Germany. In global comparison for 2020, Germany ranks in the top quartile of country size and Luxembourg in the lowest quartile.

Importantly, the case study approach allows us to move beyond variables and statistical relations between size and administrative characteristics and to dig deeper into the individual cases to probe the plausibility of their causal relationship. By focusing on a few cases, we can uncover how size effects play out in practice in these most similar countries. To do so, the section combines comparative data sources from Section 3 with primary and secondary sources on the three countries. Primary sources include government documents and interviews with public servants. In 2018 and 2019, I conducted twenty interviews, some with several respondents, about actual government practices and coordination in Luxembourg and Germany.[5] The interviewees were mostly high-level government officials, some also nongovernmental experts such as journalists. Although these interviews are not representative, they provide insights into administrators' actual motives and practices in the smallest and largest of the three cases. For the analysis, all interviews were transcribed and hand-coded by the author following a descriptive coding scheme. Secondary sources include international reports by experts and international organizations and academic literature. As typical for small states, Luxembourg is rarely considered in international scholarly research, while there is considerable academic literature about public administration in the Netherlands and Germany. However, to the best of my knowledge, none of the three has been studied systematically and academically through the analytical lens of country size. Hence, this section offers fresh insights also to those readers who are more familiar with any of these country cases. The diversity of these sources allows for triangulation and offers a detailed picture of each country's administrative system. All sources were carefully analyzed and triangulated to identify patterns and links to size. Based on this analytical approach, the section explores what difference size makes for the countries' administrative systems, structural

---

[5] For details, see Jugl (2020a, 74, 138).

and organizational particularities, systematic challenges, and performance. Following the theoretical framework, the next subsections address these questions. Figure 9 summarizes the comparative findings.

5.2 Structure

Administrative structure starts from the overall size of the administrative system. According to the latest comparable figures for the three countries (OECD 2021), total public employment in 2018 matched the overall gaps in country size: general government employees numbered about 54,800 in Luxembourg, about 1.1 million in the Netherlands, and about 4.7 million in Germany. These extreme differences in the *absolute* size of the public sector are in line with the theoretical framework. Data reveal a different pattern when it comes to the *relative* size of the public sector, public employment as a share of all employees in the country: Luxembourg has the largest public sector in relative size with 12.2 percent of total employment, the Netherlands followed with 11.7 percent, and Germany had the

Figure 9 Administrative structures, practices, and performance in three countries
Note: For sources, see text.

lowest public employment share among the three with 10.6 percent. Although these differences are small compared to other European states (Jugl 2020b, 79), they align with the general argument that smaller states have larger public sectors in relative terms. What we will focus on here, though, is the difference in absolute size that determines the degree of specialization and internal practices.

In terms of vertical specialization, the three countries are almost perfect representatives of different sizes. Small Luxembourg is a unitary-centralized state; the medium-sized Netherlands is a decentralized unitary state; and large Germany has a federal-decentralized system. The different degrees of vertical specialization are reflected in employment numbers for 2019 (OECD 2021). In Luxembourg, only 24.6 percent of general government employees worked at the subcentral level, compared to 64.8 percent in the Netherlands and 81 percent in Germany. A higher share of subnational public employees suggests that subnational governments have greater responsibilities in the provision of services and implementation of policies. In terms of size and functions, Bossaert (2018, 709) suggests that "the small and 'generalist' Luxembourgish public administration can . . . best be compared with a regional administration of a big state."

Luxembourg has two main administrative tiers, central and municipal. Policy implementation is generally centralized but municipalities have some competencies that they execute under the supervision of the Ministry of the Interior (Bossaert 2018, 696). Strong centralization is obviously linked to Luxembourg's small size (Bossaert 2018, 699); more vertical specialization would be inefficient. The Netherlands, in contrast, has a strong tradition of decentralization and an administrative system with three main levels of government: the central level, provinces, and municipalities. In practice, decentralization and recent changes favor the municipalities more than the provinces, the latter having very limited competencies. Policy implementation and public service delivery is largely left to the municipalities, although in collaboration with the central level (van der Meer 2018, 762–68).

Germany as the largest of the three has the highest degree of vertical specialization with four administrative tiers: central level (federal), states (*Länder*), counties, and municipalities. The central level is mainly in charge of policy making and funding. It has little administrative delivery capacity, except for areas like policing and immigration (Wegrich and Hammerschmid 2018, 362). The federal arrangement affords subnational states extensive competencies in lawmaking and in the execution of their own state-level policies and tasks transferred from the central level. The local level, including counties and municipalities, is also involved in implementation and works under the oversight of the *Länder* (Behnke and Kropp 2021). Responsibilities for many policy areas are shared between the central, state, and/or local level. The distribution and sharing of competencies have afforded the German system the labels of "administrative," "cooperative" and "coordinated" federalism (Behnke and Kropp 2021; Pollitt and Bouckaert 2017, 49; Wegrich and Hammerschmid 2018, 359–63). In sum, the German system is based on conflicting logics. On the one hand, there is a high degree of vertical specialization and fragmentation (Wegrich and Hammerschmid 2018, 363) based on historically rooted principles of subsidiarity and local autonomy. On the other hand, administrative cooperation and coordination across levels and the joint and uniform provision of tasks are engrained in legal frameworks and in the administrative culture (Behnke and Kropp 2021, 38–41). In sum, the three countries reflect the link between country size and vertical specialization very well.

Zooming in on the central government, we can also compare the degree of horizontal specialization in the three national administrative systems. Regarding the number of central-level government ministries, Germany has slightly more than the Netherlands, 15 compared to 12 (OECD 2019), which is in line with expectations about higher specialization. However, the case of Luxembourg does not fit with the expectations of the theoretical framework. In 2019, Luxembourg counted 24 ministries headed by 17 ministers. In an instance of small-state polyvalence, ministers in Luxembourg regularly head several ministries, which facilitates coordination between ministries and within the cabinet (Bossaert 2018, 715). The number of ministries in Luxembourg also appears less impressive when taking into account their role as the main administrative organizations in a highly centralized state. Central administrative tasks such as taxes and customs are often executed by general services closely associated with a ministry that holds direct responsibility. Reforms toward agencification have remained timid and have hardly changed the overall structure of the state. The 24 government ministries continue to be the central building blocks of the Luxembourgish administration (Bossaert 2018, 699–700; Thijs, Hammerschmid, and Palaric 2018, 18).

In contrast, both Germany and the Netherlands have considerable numbers of agencies and other central-level units, below and beside the government ministries. In both countries, the tasks of ministries are primarily policy formulation and monitoring, while administrative tasks at the central level are carried out by other units, such as agencies. In Germany, as mentioned before, service delivery is left largely to the subnational level and federal agencies mostly fulfill advisory and support functions. The majority of public employees at the central level, about 90 percent according to Fleischer (2021, 70), work at these agencies and not in the (fewer) government ministries. German central administration has, thus, a strong degree of specialization below the ministerial level. Federal agencies have grown over time without a singular political mandate to create them or a unified framework for managing them (Fleischer 2021, 70). The picture is different in the Netherlands where extensive agencification reforms informed by New Public Management, also known as "functional decentralization," changed the structure of the central administration in the 1980s and 1990s (Yesilkagit and Van Thiel 2012). Implementation tasks were reorganized into independent and semi-autonomous agencies to allow for greater managerial autonomy (van der Meer 2018, 768). Because of issues of definition and comparability, it is difficult to identify the exact number of government agencies in both countries. Bach and Huber (2012, 205) explain, however, that because the central level in the Netherlands plays a stronger role in public services, "the total number of legally independent organizations in the Netherlands is much higher than the total of organizations counted in . . . Germany."

In sum, horizontal specialization is more difficult to measure and compare across cases than vertical specialization. Luxembourg has the largest number of government ministries, but these are the main organizational units charged with policy formulation and implementation. Germany, in contrast, leaves implementation primarily to the subnational level and has a medium degree of fragmentation of ministries and agencies at the central level. The Netherlands has the most fragmented and specialized central administration due to its size (it is larger than Luxembourg) and its unitary setup (it has more administrative tasks at the central level than Germany), which leads to a very high number of central-level agencies.

Another conclusion relates to administrative reform capacity. It is well known in the comparative literature that Germany and Luxembourg are "maintainers" (Pollitt and Bouckaert 2017, 116; Toonen 2007, 303) and slow in taking up administrative reforms, whereas the Netherlands is a core "modernizer" (Pollitt and Bouckaert 2017, 117), known particularly for its extensive agencification (Bach and Huber 2012). The comparative and analytical lens of country size offers a new interpretation and explanation of these different attitudes toward reform: it is likely that we see little reform of administrative structures in Luxembourg because of size-related functional pressures. The limited resources and limited numbers of public employees do not allow further specialization, fragmentation, agencification, and the like. Senior civil servants and government ministers with a high workload across different tasks, projects, and day-to-day challenges (Bossaert 2018, 714) are not likely to focus on administrative reform or restructuring based on the latest reform narrative or trend. Germany and its structurally specialized central administration, on the other hand, may have the resources to develop reform plans, but its large size and fragmentation make the implementation of comprehensive administrative reforms difficult (Wegrich 2021). Horizontal fragmentation between ministries is entrenched in the constitution as the "departmental principle" (Fleischer 2021, 65, 75; Wegrich and Hammerschmid 2018, 363), according to which "each Federal Minister shall conduct the affairs of his department independently and on his own responsibility" (Article 65 of the Basic Law). Together with the strong role and involvement of the states in administrative matters, this hinders the adoption of government-wide reforms. Finally, the medium size of the Netherlands seems to be conducive to centralized administrative reform. On the one hand, medium size and the lack of a strong regional level implies a certain need for specialization, which was addressed through spatial (vertical) decentralization and functional decentralization (agencification). On the other hand, medium size and a medium degree of fragmentation within a unitary system afford the government center the capacity and authority to implement major system-level reform initiatives (van der Meer 2018, 763–65, 779). These considerations also apply to changes and inertia in recruitment and management practices.

5.3 Practices

This subsection discusses administrative practices, first related to personnel management and then related to coordination. Generally speaking, all three countries follow the Weberian virtues of professionalism and meritocracy. They recruit public servants based on merit and through a formal process, and all three systems achieve high scores of professionalism in international rankings. Comparing public personnel and human resource management (HRM) practices across the three countries, we still find subtle differences. The Netherlands start from a traditional position-based system, where civil servants have to apply for a new position to move up, but the country also has some career elements at the central level. Germany and Luxembourg started, and largely remained, on a career-based trajectory characterized by "closed recruitment policy, seniority-based promotion and low accessibility for lateral entrants" (Thijs, Hammerschmid, and Palaric 2018, 24). In the strict sense, these different starting points violate the most similar systems assumption underlying the comparison. In a broader sense, they highlight that idiosyncratic historical factors condition the paths that countries are taking, besides and beyond the effects of size. Accounting for these differences in starting points, the three cases still reflect a different propensity and capacity for reform similar to the patterns discussed for administrative structures.

The Netherlands is moving in line with the international trend toward position-based and more open civil service systems (Thijs, Hammerschmid, and Palaric 2018, 24), and reform debates are ongoing (van der Meer 2018, 769). There are efforts to decrease government fragmentation and increase coordination through the creation of a coherent and mobile Senior Public Service (ABD in Dutch) with a focus on management rather than legal skills. Other reforms aim to standardize HRM practices across central government ministries (van der Meer 2018, 769–70). This flexible combination of elements – position- and career-based, traditional and innovative – reflects the Dutch capacity and willingness for HRM reform in order to increase administrative performance.

Germany and Luxembourg, instead, have held on to their career-based systems and introduced only limited HRM reforms. In Germany (Reichard and Schröter 2021; Wegrich and Hammerschmid 2018, 368–74), strong and "rigid" (Wegrich and Hammerschmid 2018, 371) career-based elements exist for civil servants and public employees. The large size and decentralization of administrative tasks result in some variation of HRM practices at the *Länder* level, but overall, a strong commitment to formal rules and traditional practices persists. In particular, the selection and education of public servants still have a strong focus on legal skills and application of law rather than a focus on performance and managerial skills as in the Netherlands. In sum, the German public personnel system has proved remarkably stable. Reichard and Schröter (2021, 219) argue that this continuity is based on a strong legal and constitutional foundation of key principles, on the decentralized and fragmented nature of the administrative system, and on the highly organized interests of civil servants and public employees. These three reasons are all in line with the theoretical framework as they reflect formalization, fragmentation, and a critical mass of bureaucrats in a large state.

Luxembourg, instead, achieves a high degree of professionalism *despite* its small size. The country retains one of the most traditional career-based systems in Europe. Professionalism and merit-based recruitment are ensured through an extremely centralized process based on central competitive exams organized by the Ministry of Civil Service and approval by the Prime Minister (Bossaert 2018, 702–4). Besides this professional system, Luxembourg's HRM displays some small-state characteristics. Individual bureaucrats typically work on several projects or dossiers (Högenauer 2016, 95). Luxembourg has been more flexible and pragmatic than Germany in adapting existing rules and practices, without going down the Dutch road of comprehensive reform. Faced with a limited human resource pool and changes in the environment, Luxembourg's administration pragmatically opened up to the recruitment of experts with private-sector experience, for example, in the field of digitalization

(Bossaert 2018, 702, 705). However, against the theoretical expectation, the small size of the public service does not preclude a distinct bureaucratic identity and a strong institutionalization of public servants' interests. There is a union and the elected Chamber of Civil Servants and State Employees to represent their interests in social dialogue with the Luxembourgish government (Bossaert 2018, 705).

Finally, politicization of the public service is limited in all three countries. Van der Meer (2018, 772) argues that it is virtually absent in the Netherlands, which suggests highest levels of meritocracy. In Luxembourg, government ministers at the head of a ministry can typically appoint one or two advisors and propose other senior civil servants from inside the civil service (Bossaert 2018, 704–5). In Germany, politicization in ministries may be regarded as "medium" (Wegrich and Hammerschmid 2018, 374) because ministers can typically appoint "political civil servants" at the top two levels of their ministry: administrative state secretaries and heads of directorates. However, taking into account the large size of Germany and its (central) administration as well as the more complex intra-ministerial hierarchies, the share of politically appointed civil servants seems very small, as in Luxembourg.

Moving on to coordination practices, we can observe further differences related to size. There is evidence of greater need for, and greater challenges to, coordination in the large and fragmented German system. The midsize Netherlands has also recognized the need for better coordination, especially within its specialized central administration, but it has been rather successful with centralized, formal and informal, approaches to coordination. Debates are very different in small Luxembourg, where informal practices contribute to a high degree of coordination of government action.

In Germany, horizontal and vertical fragmentation and the strong inter-dependencies between administrative units and levels lead to a very high need for coordination. This need is amplified by the administrative culture and its emphasis on cooperation and coordination. Scharpf (1988) has argued famously that high fragmentation and a strong will to coordinate jointly lead to the "joint decision trap" resulting in deadlock or lowest denominator outcomes. Therefore, the actual coordination quality in the German government and administration is medium in comparative perspective (Thijs, Hammerschmid, and Palaric 2018, 34). The main tools for coordination are formal meetings, committees, and the like. Vertical coordination (Behnke and Kropp 2021, 42–46) between the central level and the state level occurs through the second parliamentary chamber, the *Bundesrat*, and its committees. From a public administration perspective, it is important that the *Bundesrat* is formed by *Länder* governments with a direct link to the subnational administrations.

Most of its committees are composed of higher-ranking civil servants from the respective state administrations. Further committees and working groups such as the conference of state ministers coordinate policies and implementation horizontally between the *Länder* and are sometimes open to representatives from the central government as well. At the central level, the Chancellery as the center of government is formally in charge of horizontal coordination between ministries. Typical formats besides the cabinet and the cabinet preparation are temporary working groups or the appointment of federal commissioners (Wegrich and Hammerschmid 2018, 365). The backbone of inter-ministerial coordination is the co-signature procedure formalized in the government's procedural rules (GGO in German), according to which a lead ministry formulates a policy proposal and consults with any other ministry with jurisdictions affected by the bill (Fleischer 2021, 71).

Why does this sophisticated system of coordination practices in Germany lead only to mediocre results? In line with the literature on bureaucratic pathologies and the argument that they are driven by large size and specialization, the German administration suffers from marked silo thinking and rival identities between government levels, ministries, and agencies. The departmental principle and departmental autonomy, together with the lack of mobility of public servants between organizations, reinforce horizontal fragmentation and hinder effective coordination. Asked why coordination and cooperation are so difficult in practice, an interviewee from a German government ministry shrugged and responded, "every ministry has its pride." At the same time, overlapping jurisdictions can lead to unclear responsibilities and to "blame games," as another interviewee in the federal administration said. The size, closedness, and autonomy of ministries nurture distinct and rival identities and make coordination particularly difficult for the Chancellery compared to other European centers of government (Wegrich and Hammerschmid 2018, 365). The strong focus on formal roles, rules, and piecemeal tasks is another important barrier to coordination. Based on the dominance of legal training and perspectives in the German administration, there is often little focus on overarching policy goals or results. The size of administrative organizations and formalized procedures also prescribe rigid and hierarchical communication channels and prevent horizontal exchanges at the working level across different ministries or agencies. Finally, the co-signature procedure is a highly formalized routine that often results in negative coordination (Bouckaert, Peters, and Verhoest 2010, 20; Mayntz and Scharpf 1975). Ministries simply check whether a new policy would violate their turf or interests, but there is rarely any "constructive" or "positive" coordination in the sense of joint policy formulation by several ministries.

Compared to Germany, administration in the Netherlands has features we would expect given its medium size. There is somewhat less but still considerable need for coordination, especially at the fragmented central level of the Dutch government. At the same time, the Dutch system has developed effective practices to address this need and reach high coordination quality (Thijs, Hammerschmid, and Palaric 2018, 34). Based on a tradition of central-level specialization and ministerial responsibility, compartmentalization has been recognized as a central problem of Dutch administration since the 1970s (Bouckaert, Peters, and Verhoest 2010, 153). Subsequent governments pursued different strategies to tackle this problem. Examples include increased informal consultations among top-level ministerial bureaucrats since the 1980s (Bouckaert, Peters, and Verhoest 2010, 158), the creation of the government-wide senior civil service with interdepartmental mobility and shared norms in the 1990s (van der Meer 2018, 770), and interdepartmental peer reviews introduced in 2001 (Bouckaert, Peters, and Verhoest 2010, 165). Although the Prime Minister and the Prime Minister's office have relatively weak coordination capacities, most of these efforts were top-down, initiated primarily by ministers of the interior or finance (Bouckaert, Peters, and Verhoest 2010, 275). A success factor was that rules and structures were understood as means of achieving results, not as ends in themselves as in Germany. In terms of policy coordination, the drafting of proposals can be allocated to one or two lead ministries in the Netherlands. Coordination of proposals and pre-proposal ideas takes place through formal and informal channels, although not without certain elements of negative coordination (SGI 2020, 29, 45–46); "informal coordination and the personal chemistry among civil servants are what keeps things running" (SGI 2020, 89). This illustrates the pragmatic mix of formal and informal coordination practices in the Netherlands.

By virtue of Luxembourg's small size, its comparatively low fragmentation and specialization pose a much smaller challenge for coordination. Besides the cabinet and the informal pre-cabinet meetings of senior civil servants, there are no formal interdepartmental coordination mechanisms (SGI 2020, 15, 29) and still, Luxembourg achieves comparatively high coordination quality (Thijs, Hammerschmid, and Palaric 2018, 34). The working style in central ministries can be described as "pragmatic" (Bossaert 2018, 700). Because units and individuals have to cover several topics and because units are small, they do not lose sight of overarching goals and are less prone to develop silo thinking or rivalries. Typical of small states, individuals in the Luxembourgish administration have considerable room for maneuver; for example, senior civil servants "run the [EU] negotiations relatively independently" (Högenauer 2016, 94). This requires a good overview of relevant topics and government positions, and it differs from the narrow tasks and responsibilities found especially in the German administration. A recently introduced practice of management by objectives reinforces the coherence between macro-, meso-, and micro-level goals in Luxembourg: political priorities and goals "are cascaded down from organizational level to individual level during individual staff interviews" (Bossaert 2018, 703). With an explicit emphasis on strengthening motivation and performance, this practice formalizes the coordination between individual tasks and policy objectives that has "naturally" existed before (MFP 2020).

In terms of inter-ministerial coordination, results from the interviews about actual government practices and coordination in Luxembourg are telling. In all interviews with high-level public servants, elements or traces of interministerial conflict were completely absent. This is in stark contrast to interviews with their German counterparts. What surfaced repeatedly in these interviews and what further facilitates coordination in Luxembourg are pervasive informal communication and personal relations. With regard to the country's small size, one ministry official said, "I'd say it's a strength after all, because basically everybody knows everybody." Other civil servants said that they have known their counterparts in other ministries or government politicians from various encounters in the private and professional realm, for example, from their childhood, high school, a shared student job, or previous joint projects. This familiarity speeds up communication, often by skipping formal communication channels. When issues occur during policy formulation or administrative implementation, civil servants often pick up the phone to call whomever they believe can help solve the issue, be it a senior bureaucrat or minister. This means that informal contacts and communication facilitate coordination within ministries and horizontally, between ministries. Organizational boundaries are much less inhibiting than in Germany or the Netherlands. The findings from the interviews coincide with expert assessments (Bossaert 2018; SGI 2020) that highlight the positive role of informal coordination and of overlapping professional and private roles for coordination outcomes: "Additional cabinet committees do not seem necessary as there are ad hoc meetings between relevant ministers on specific issues. The system is not rigid or predetermined, but works well" (SGI 2020, 45).

The discussion of HRM and coordination practices in the three countries has revealed "formality" versus "informality and pragmatism" as an underlying dimension of these practices that is strongly determined by size. Although Luxembourg and Germany both adhere to a traditional procedural approach to administrative practices (Thijs, Hammerschmid, and Palaric 2018, 36), Luxembourg implements this approach more pragmatically and flexibly. The Netherlands instead has moved to a managerial logic that combines formal and informal practices with the goal of achieving good results. These findings match well with the central administrative values of each system: impartiality, neutrality, and independence in Luxembourg (Bossaert 2018, 709); effectiveness, efficiency, and fairness in the Netherlands (van der Meer 2018, 774); and legality, impartiality and equality in Germany (Wegrich and Hammerschmid 2018, 378). Although all three sets of values highlight aspects of equal and fair treatment of citizens, there are slight but important variations. The Luxembourgish values portray an administration that aims to achieve Weberian professionalism, while the Dutch values focus on results and the German ones put legal procedures first.

5.4 Performance

How do these different structures and practices play out in terms of performance and quality of the public administration? In the World Bank's Government Effectiveness index (Kaufmann, Kraay, and Mastruzzi 2009), all three countries are highly ranked. However, in recent years, Germany has scored consistently lower than the other two, and the Netherlands has continuously reached the highest scores in at least the 96th percentile in global comparison. In 2020, Germany reached a score of 1.36, while Luxembourg scored 1.84 and the Netherlands scored 1.85. In terms of citizen satisfaction with public services reported in the Eurobarometer survey (European Commission 2019), the rank order of the three countries is the same. The highest satisfaction is reached in the Netherlands with 91 percent of respondents judging the public service provision as "good" or "very good," compared to 89 percent in Luxembourg and 74 percent in Germany.

Digitalization and transparency are of growing interest in relation to administrative performance. Here, the Netherlands again outperforms the other two countries on several indicators ranging from e-government users to user-centricity and open data. This results in an overall Digital Public Services score of 81 in the Netherlands, compared to 74 in Luxembourg and 66 in Germany (European Commission 2020). These scores reflect again the countries' differences in administrative structures and practices. Dutch government authorities have formulated a joint, government-wide vision for digital service provision since as early as 2010 (van der Meer 2018, 777). This strategy is radically citizen-centered and aims to "not bother citizens, entrepreneurs and institutions with the differences between our [government] organizations: we operate as one government."[6] Luxembourg started from a laggard position but

---

[6] www.digitaleoverheid.nl/overzicht-van-alle-onderwerpen/archief/beleid/ (accessed November 5, 2021)

has considerably improved in recent years because of centralized digitalization efforts (Bossaert 2018, 713–14; European Commission 2020). Germany's comparably poor performance is linked to horizontal and vertical fragmentation of administration, limited cooperation, and a lack of effective steering at the federal level, which all impede government-wide reform (Wegrich 2021; Wegrich and Hammerschmid 2018, 366, 382).

Taken together, these performance indicators suggest that Germany is larger than the "golden mean" of optimum country size and that problems linked to extreme fragmentation and bureaucratic pathologies limit its overall administrative performance when it comes to non-routine tasks. The medium-sized Netherlands, which combines medium degrees of specialization with formal and informal coordination practices, currently achieves the highest administrative performance and quality of the three. Luxembourg's higher per capita GDP may play a role in the country's very strong performance that comes close to the Netherlands', despite the very small country size that hardly allows for economies of scale. In sum, this section has elaborated on how size effects play out in the administrative structures, practices, and performance in three comparable European states. It has demonstrated the analytical value of the theoretical framework and a country-size perspective that draws attention to the very distinct challenges and opportunities in three countries that the literature typically categorizes in the same group of administrative systems.

6 Conclusion and Research Agenda

This Element has introduced country size to comparative public administration. I have demonstrated how size matters for the organization and functioning of public administration. To that end, I have developed a theoretical framework that synthesizes existing literature and that is unprecedentedly comprehensive and detailed. It allows us to distinguish between size effects for administrative structure, practices, and performance. It shows that country size does not only have "mechanical" effects on structure and specialization but can also have more subtle effects on identities, communication, and practices, which are more difficult to theorize and to observe. Considering the various advantages and disadvantages of small and large sizes, the framework predicts a curvilinear relationship between country size and public service performance. A central theoretical contribution is the explicit conceptualization of ideal-typical features of public administration in midsize and large countries.

Empirically, this Element has presented three different research approaches to explore country size effects on public administration. All of them employ a form of cross-country comparison, which is necessary for studying the effects of country size. None of them is without limitations, but their combination provides a powerful and multifaceted view on size effects. The section on indicators and correlations provides the first comprehensive mapping of administrative structures, practices, and performances along the global variation of population size. Given the novelty of the topic, this descriptive approach is both useful and needed; however, the bivariate perspective is too limited to identify size effects clearly. To distinguish the effect of population size from other factors, the section on causal statistical analysis includes several important control variables, such as GDP per capita, democracy, and a proxy for administrative traditions. Furthermore, it employs several modeling strategies to isolate the effect of country size and estimate the "golden mean." This is only possible by focusing on one outcome, government effectiveness. The third empirical section takes a different approach by zooming in on three most similar country cases and exploring the various ways in which differences in size play out in administrative practices and reform trajectories over time.

The main conclusion from these analyses is that size matters. Comparative public administration can become analytically stronger by recognizing important differences between countries it has often regarded as similar. For instance, the largest OECD country, the United States, is about 900 times larger in terms of population than the smallest OECD member Iceland, and this difference affects public administration in several ways. Country size should be added to the list of important contextual factors that public managers and public administration scholars should keep in mind when analyzing or designing administrative structures and processes (Ongaro, Gong, and Jing 2021; O'Toole Jr. and Meier 2017). Size is a contextual meta factor that shapes several other contextual factors under which public administration operates, including dispersion of political power, turbulence and external pressures, resource endowment, goal clarity, and formalization. Importantly, country size is not only an important environmental factor for small states, as has often been assumed, but it is also at work in medium and large states.

To take context seriously means to pay attention to it, for example, when adopting a management practice from another country and context. Section 5 has illustrated the particular challenges but also strategies in countries of varying sizes; this has hopefully contributed to a deeper understanding among scholars and practitioners of the implications of size. As inspiration for public management and administrative reform, practitioners should look to countries of similar size. An example of best practices in small states is related to the small island states in the Caribbean: to overcome structural limitations of smallness, they pool their limited resources at a supranational level in the

Organization for Eastern Caribbean States (OECS), and this allows them to jointly offer specialized training to public servants as well as professional monetary and regulatory policies. At a more abstract level, this Element has demonstrated that macro-level questions in public administration (Roberts 2020) are of enduring importance and practical relevance. In Dahl's (1947) sense, research on country size can be understood as comparative and "basic" research that contributes to a better understanding of practical problems of administration on the ground.

One goal of this Element was to develop a research agenda around this emerging topic. Although the literature has advanced over the last years, there are important things that we do not know yet about size and public administration. First of all, the external validity of the arguments about size and administration deserves more study. This Element has pushed the empirical boundaries of the literature by looking beyond small states and by including medium and large states in quantitative and qualitative analyses. It has also explicitly included non-Western and non-democratic states in the statistical analyses, settings that are often overlooked in the public administration literature. While the hypothesized size effect on performance found support in a global sample, it was not found in a subsample of nondemocratic states. Future studies should further explore whether and why size effects hold, or not, in various geographic and political contexts.

A second avenue for future research is to think about the substantial policy implications of differences in size and administration. I have used aggregate and general measures of administrative performance. Future studies could employ more actionable and policy-specific performance indicators to explore if and how size-induced variation in the capacity to formulate, coordinate, and implement policy affects actual policy outcomes on the ground. There is much work to be done in order to assess the degree to which size influences variation in policy performance (see Anckar 2020).

Studying administrative outcomes and public policies in small countries can offer important insights for larger states as well. Small states can be understood as policy laboratories where policies are tested under particularly tough conditions: if policies succeed in small states, where public administration as well as organizations in the private and nonprofit sector face limited resources, very limited numbers of users or customers, and a lack of economies of scale, then these policies may be promising in other contexts as well. Extreme conditions, which have long been typical of small states, mirror some of the most pressing challenges that larger states are increasingly facing, such as austerity, dependence on volatile world markets, or the effects of climate change. For such policy experimentation and knowledge transfer to succeed, we must better tease out the lessons that small states offer to larger states. There is an abundance of case studies about small state policies, for example, in the field of climate and the environment, but this scholarship does not yet speak to mainstream academia nor to practitioners in larger states. Thus, a better synthesis of such findings is needed.

However, focusing on substantive effects does not only require more empirical work but also theory. Size is likely to affect policy outcomes but probably in diverse ways. Future research could disentangle the differential effects that size can have on different types of policy issues and outcomes and on different decision making processes. Again, the small state literature offers interesting starting points that are ready for more systematic testing and comparative study *across* the size continuum. This literature has argued that small states are better able than larger ones to adapt flexibly to changing economic pressures and external challenges, precisely because they have been exposed to such challenging environments for a long time (Katzenstein 1985). In more theoretical terms, the meta context of smallness produces a context of turbulence that may *positively* affect performance. This "paradox of vulnerability" (Campbell and Hall 2017) builds on closely knitted national communities and a feeling of "everyone sitting in the same boat," which arguably leads to more internal solidarity and long-term orientation in smaller states. The idea of policy flexibility also links to the argument that small states and their multifunctional administrations are better able to avoid silo-thinking and to see the big picture (Sarapuu and Randma-Liiv 2020, 58). Policy flexibility may be linked, finally, to political science arguments about veto points and veto players. As we have seen with the autonomy of subnational units, institutional specialization is weaker in small states, which may result in fewer veto points and quicker and more flexible decision making (Dahl and Tufte 1973). Through these channels, country size may affect how governments address pressing issues, such as urgent crises, but also long-term policy changes and adaptation.

Future studies could theorize if such effects are continuous along the country-size spectrum and if we should expect the opposite, namely policy rigidity, in large states – or if these arguments apply exclusively to very small states. We may also ask for which types of policy issues such beneficial effects of smallness outweigh the disadvantages, and vice versa. Policy flexibility may be limited to those policy fields that have traditionally been subject to external pressures, like (macro-)economic policy. Multifunctionalism and limited specialization may be beneficial for policy issues including wicked problems that require attention to broader developments that cut across traditional ministerial boundaries and that receive such attention and prioritization in a small-state administration and government. On the other hand, negative effects of smallness, and hence worse policy performance than in larger states, may prevail for issues that either have a lower priority in small-state administrations, perhaps due to a lack of perceived vulnerability, or that need a lot of technical expertise. These points should be investigated, for example, by comparing actual policy making or crisis management processes in small and large states. Exploring these links may also offer interesting lessons for researchers and practitioners in medium and large states about how to foster adaptation to a fast-changing world.

The argument about small states' policy flexibility stands in contrast to the observation that small states are particularly conservative in terms of state and societal structures and institutions (Corbett, Veenendaal, and Ugyel 2017, 690, 692; Lowenthal 1987, 35). This paradox is well reflected in the case of Luxembourg where we saw little formal changes in administrative structures but a flexible use and application of those structures to changing circumstances. Future research may explore the differences in capacity for administrative reform and for policy change between small, medium, and large countries. Uncovering and explaining such differences, and potential interactions between institutional stability and policy flexibility, will have implications for countries of either size.

Comparative public administration research and the study of size effects, in particular, may also benefit from taking a long-term perspective. Given that administrative features as well as country size are slowly changing and "sticky" over time, a historical perspective will allow researchers to uncover how the two co-evolved over time, perhaps over centuries. The increasing availability of comparative and historical data sets in political science is promising for such analysis. This would shed light on an issue that is of theoretical and methodological importance for research on size effects: the survival of countries over time and the endogeneity of country size. Why have certain small states survived over time despite adversarial circumstances and external threats? Why, on the other hand, have certain larger states survived and managed their internal diversity while others have fallen apart? Exploring these macro-level historical trajectories will help us understand which types of historical small and large countries have survived until today and along which survival criteria. In these cases, we may then explore the stabilizing role of state structures, administrative practices, and results. Less successful cases of failed countries may offer historical lessons on administrative pathologies.

Finally, a question that combines several of the previous points and which deserves more attention is this: Why do some medium-sized countries perform particularly badly in global comparison, even when taking political and economic factors into account? Under which conditions do the best of both worlds really come together? And how do some small states overcome their structural limitations and outperform larger ones? We still lack a good understanding of why small or medium size is sometimes good and sometimes bad. Future research should explore the respective scope conditions. In theoretical terms, this points to the interaction between size and other contextual factors. This suggests that context is much more complex than how it is often portrayed in the public administration literature. Context is not a binary variable, something that is either present or absent, but it is in itself the combination and interaction of various aspects that are internal and external to public sector organizations. Exploring this interaction calls for more genuinely comparative research and a fruitful combination of in-depth case studies and systematic cross-case, and perhaps longitudinal, comparisons. With this Element, I have aimed to stimulate such debates and to highlight the relevance of comparative perspectives and methods in public administration research.

References

Alesina, Alberto, Reza Baqir, and William Easterly. 1999. "Public Goods and Ethnic Divisions." *The Quarterly Journal of Economics* 114 (4): 1243–84.

Alesina, Alberto, Arnaud Devleeschauwer, William Easterly, Sergio Kurlat, and Romain Wacziarg. 2003. "Fractionalization." *Journal of Economic Growth* 8 (2): 155–94.

Alesina, Alberto, and Enrico Spolaore. 2005. *The Size of Nations*. Cambridge: The MIT Press.

Alesina, Alberto, and Romain Wacziarg. 1998. "Openness, Country Size and Government." *Journal of Public Economics* 69 (3): 305–21.

Anckar, Dag. 2020. "Small States: Politics and Policies." In *Handbook on the Politics of Small States*, edited by Godfrey Baldacchino and Anders Wivel, 38–54. Cheltenham: Edward Elgar.

Anderson, Derrick M., and Justin M. Stritch. 2016. "Goal Clarity, Task Significance, and Performance: Evidence From a Laboratory Experiment." *Journal of Public Administration Research and Theory* 26 (2): 211–25.

Andrews, Rhys, and George A. Boyne. 2009. "Size, Structure and Administrative Overheads: An Empirical Analysis of English Local Authorities." *Urban Studies* 46 (4): 739–59.

Andrews, Rhys, Malcolm J. Beynon, and Aoife M. McDermott. 2016. "Organizational Capability in the Public Sector: A Configurational Approach." *Journal of Public Administration Research and Theory* 26 (2): 239–58.

Bach, Tobias, and Etienne Huber. 2012. "Comparing Agencification in Continental Countries." In *Government Agencies: Practices and Lessons from 30 Countries*, edited by Koen Verhoest, Sandra Van Thiel, Geert Bouckaert, and Per Lægreid, 203–10. Public Sector Organizations. Basingstoke [et al.]: Palgrave Macmillan.

Bach, Tobias, and Kai Wegrich. 2019. "Blind Spots, Biased Attention, and the Politics of Non-Coordination." In *The Blind Spots of Public Bureaucracy and the Politics of Non-Coordination*, edited by Tobias Bach and Kai Wegrich, 3–28. Cham: Palgrave Macmillan.

Bäck, Hanna, and Axel Hadenius. 2008. "Democracy and State Capacity: Exploring a J-Shaped Relationship." *Governance* 21 (1): 1–24.

Bartels, Brandon. 2008. "Beyond 'Fixed versus Random Effects': A Framework for Improving Substantive and Statistical Analysis of

Panel, Time-Series Cross-Sectional, and Multilevel Data." *Paper Presented at the Political Methodology Conference. Ann Arbor, MI. 9–12 July*, 1–43.

Behnke, Nathalie, and Sabine Kropp. 2021. "Administrative Federalism." In *Public Administration in Germany*, edited by Sabine Kuhlmann, Isabella Proeller, Dieter Schimanke, Jan Ziekow, 35–51. Cham: Palgrave Macmillan.

Bell, Andrew, and Kelvyn Jones. 2015. "Explaining Fixed Effects: Random Effects Modeling of Time-Series Cross-Sectional and Panel Data." *Political Science Research and Methods* 3 (1): 133–53.

Benedict, Burton. 1966. "Sociological Characteristics of Small Territories and Their Implications for Economic Development." In *The Social Anthropology of Complex Societies*, edited by Michael Banton, 23–36. London: Tavistock.

ed. 1967. *Problems of Smaller Territories*. London: Athlone.

Bernauer, Julian, and Adrian Vatter. 2017. "Conflict, Choice or Geography? Explaining Patterns of Democracy in Continental Europe." *European Journal of Political Research* 56 (2): 251–78.

Bertelli, Anthony M., Mai Hassan, Dan Honig, Daniel Rogger, and Martin J. Williams. 2020. "An Agenda for the Study of Public Administration in Developing Countries." *Governance* 33 (4): 735–48.

Bertels, Jana, and Lena Schulze-Gabrechten. 2021. "Mapping the Black Box of Intraministerial Organization: An Analytical Approach to Explore Structural Diversity below the Portfolio Level." *Governance* 34 (1): 171–89.

Bjørnskov, Christian. 2010. "How Does Social Trust Lead to Better Governance? An Attempt to Separate Electoral and Bureaucratic Mechanisms." *Public Choice* 144 (1): 323–46.

Blau, Peter M. 1970. "A Formal Theory of Differentiation in Organizations." *American Sociological Review* 35 (2): 201–18.

Blom-Hansen, Jens, Kurt Houlberg, and Søren Serritzlew. 2014. "Size, Democracy, and the Economic Costs of Running the Political System." *American Journal of Political Science* 58 (4): 790–803.

Bossaert, Danielle. 2018. "Luxembourg." Public Administration Characteristics and Performance in EU28. Brussels: European Commission. https://op.europa.eu/en/publication-detail/-/publication/8642fbd3-9610-11e8-8bc1-01aa75ed71a1/language-en

Bouckaert, Geert, B. Guy Peters, and Koen Verhoest. 2010. *The Coordination of Public Sector Organizations*. Hampshire: Palgrave Macmillan.

Boyne, George. 1995. "Population Size and Economies of Scale in Local Government." *Policy & Politics* 23 (3): 213–22.

Bräutigam, Deborah, and Michael Woolcock. 2001. "Small States in a Global Economy." UNU/WIDER Discussion Paper No. 2001/37.

Bromfield, Nicholas, and Allan McConnell. 2021. "Two Routes to Precarious Success: Australia, New Zealand, COVID-19 and the Politics of Crisis Governance." *International Review of Administrative Sciences* 87(3): 518–35.

Campbell, John L., and John A. Hall. 2017. *The Paradox of Vulnerability: States, Nationalism, and the Financial Crisis*. Princeton, NJ: Princeton University Press.

Cerulo, Karen A. 2006. *Never Saw It Coming: Cultural Challenges to Envisioning the Worst*. Chicago: University of Chicago Press.

CIA: *The World Factbook* 2021. Washington, DC: Central Intelligence Agency. https://www.cia.gov/the-world-factbook/

Congdon Fors, Heather. 2014. "Do Island States Have Better Institutions?" *Journal of Comparative Economics* 42 (1): 34–60.

Corbett, Jack. 2015. "'Everybody Knows Everybody': Practising Politics in the Pacific Islands." *Democratization* 22 (1): 51–72.

Corbett, Jack, and Wouter P. Veenendaal. 2018. *Democracy in Small States: Persisting against All Odds*. Oxford: Oxford University Press.

Corbett, Jack, Wouter Veenendaal, and John Connell. 2021. "The Core Executive and Small States: Is Coordination the Primary Challenge?" *Public Administration* 99 (1): 103–17.

Corbett, Jack, Wouter P. Veenendaal, and Lhawang Ugyel. 2017. "Why Monarchy Persists in Small States: The Cases of Tonga, Bhutan and Liechtenstein." *Democratization* 24 (4): 689–706.

Crowards, Tom. 2002. "Defining the Category of 'small' States." *Journal of International Development* 14 (2): 143.

Dahl, Robert A. 1947. "The Science of Public Administration: Three Problems." *Public Administration Review* 7 (1): 1–11.

Dahl, Robert A., and Edward R. Tufte. 1973. *Size and Democracy*. Stanford: Stanford University Press.

Dahlström, Carl, Victor Lapuente, and Jan Teorell. 2012. "The Merit of Meritocratization: Politics, Bureaucracy, and the Institutional Deterrents of Corruption." *Political Research Quarterly* 65(3): 656–68.

Demmke, Christoph, and Timo Moilanen. 2010. *Civil Services in the EU of 27: Reform Outcomes and the Future of the Civil Service*. Frankfurt am Main: Peter Lang.

Diamond, Larry, and Svetlana Tsalik. 1999. "Size and Democracy: The Case for Decentralization." In *Developing Democracy. Toward Consolidation,* edited by Larry Diamond, 117–60. Baltimore: John Hopkins University Press.

Downs, Anthony. 1967. *Inside Bureaucracy*. A Rand Corporation Research Study. Prospect Heights: Waveland Press.

Dumont, Patrick, and Frédéric Varone. 2006. "Delegation and Accountability in Parliamentary Democracies. Smallness, Proximity and Short Cuts." In *Delegation in Contemporary Democracies*, edited by Dietmar Braun and Fabrizio Gilardi, 52–76. Abingdon: Routledge.

Durkheim, Emile. 1893. *The Division of Labor in Society*. New York: Free Press.

Easterly, William, and Aart Kraay. 2000. "Small States, Small Problems? Income, Growth, and Volatility in Small States." *World Development* 28 (11): 2013–27.

Egeberg, Morten. 1999. "The Impact of Bureaucratic Structure on Policy Making." *Public Administration* 77 (1): 155–70.

European Commission. 2019. "Public Opinion in the European Union. Report." Standard Eurobarometer 91. https://europa.eu/eurobarometer/surveys/detail/2253

——— 2020. "Digital Economy and Society Index." DESI Report 2020. https://digital-strategy.ec.europa.eu/de/node/9773

Evans, Peter, and James E. Rauch. 1999. "Bureaucracy and Growth: A Cross-National Analysis of the Effects of ' Weberian' State Structures on Economic Growth." *American Sociological Review*, 64(5):748–65.

Farrugia, Charles. 1993. "The Special Working Environment of Senior Administrators in Small States." *World Development* 21 (2): 221–26.

Fleischer, Julia. 2021. "Federal Administration." In *Public Administration in Germany*, edited by Sabine Kuhlmann, Isabella Proeller, Dieter Schimanke, Jan Ziekow, 61–79. Cham: Palgrave Macmillan.

Fligstein, Neil, Jonah Stuart Brundage, and Michael Schultz. 2017. "Seeing like the Fed: Culture, Cognition, and Framing in the Failure to Anticipate the Financial Crisis of 2008." *American Sociological Review* 82 (5): 879–909.

Gellner, Ernest. 1973. "Scale and Nation." *Philosophy of the Social Sciences* 3 (1): 1–17.

Gerring, John, Jillian Jaeger, and Matthew Maguire. 2016. "A General Theory of Power Concentration: Demographic Influences on Political Organization." Working Paper Series 29. Gothenburg: V-Dem Institute.

Gerring, John, and Matthew Maguire. 2014. "People and Power: Demographic Influences on the Organization of States." Working Paper. Boston University.

Gerring, John, Matthew Maguire, and Jillian Jaeger. 2018. "A General Theory of Power Concentration: Demographic Influences on Political Organization." *European Political Science Review* 10 (4): 491–513.

Gerring, John, and Wouter Veenendaal. 2020. *Population and Politics: The Impact of Scale*. Cambridge: Cambridge University Press.

Gingrich, Andre, and Ulf Hannerz. 2017. "Introduction: Exploring Small Countries." In *Small Countries: Structures and Sensibilities*, edited by Ulf Hannerz and Andre Gingrich, 1–44. Philadelphia: University of Pennsylvania Press.

Goertz, Gary. 2006. *Social Science Concepts: A User's Guide*. Princeton, NJ: Princeton University Press.

Grindle, Merilee S. 2012. *Jobs for the Boys. Patronage and the State in Comparative Perspective*. Cambridge [et al.]: Harvard University Press.

Habyarimana, James, Macartan Humphreys, Daniel N. Posner, and Jeremy M. Weinstein. 2007. "Why Does Ethnic Diversity Undermine Public Goods Provision?" *American Political Science Review* 101 (4): 709–25.

Halperin, Morton H., Joseph T. Siegle, and Michael M. Weinstein. 2010. *The Democracy Advantage: How Democracy Promotes Prosperity and Peace*. Revised. The Council on Foreign Relations. New York [et al.]: Routledge.

Harari, Michael B., David E. L. Herst, Heather R. Parola, and Bruce P. Carmona. 2017. "Organizational Correlates of Public Service Motivation: A Meta-Analysis of Two Decades of Empirical Research." *Journal of Public Administration Research and Theory* 27 (1): 68–84.

Hart, Paul t', and Anchrit Wille. 2012. "Bureaucratic Politics: Opening the Black Box of Executive Government." In *The Sage Handbook of Public Administration*, edited by B. Guy Peters and Jon Pierre, 2nd ed., 369–79. London: SAGE.

Högenauer, Anna-Lena. 2016. "Luxembourg's EU Council Presidency: Adapting Routines to New Circumstances." *Journal of Common Market Studies* 54: 91–100.

Hood, Christopher. 1974. "Administrative Diseases: Some Types of Dysfunctionality in Administration." *Public Administration* 52 (4): 439–54.

Hooghe, Liesbet, and Gary Marks. 2013. "Beyond Federalism: Estimating and Explaining the Territorial Structure of Government." *Publius: The Journal of Federalism* 43 (2): 179–204.

Hooghe, Liesbet, Gary Marks, Arjan H. Schakel, et al. 2016. *Measuring Regional Authority: A Postfunctionalist Theory of Governance*. Oxford: Oxford University Press.

Hooghe, Liesbet, Gary Marks, Arjan H. Schakel, et al. 2021. "Regional Authority Index (RAI) v.3." EUI Research Data. Robert Schuman Centre for Advanced Studies. Retrieved from Cadmus, European University Institute Research Repository.

ILO. 2021. "Public Employment by Sectors and Sub-Sectors of National Accounts." International Labour Organization. www.ilo.org/shinyapps/bulk explorer53/?lang=en&segment=indicator&id=PSE_TPSE_GOV_NB_A

Jann, Werner, and Kai Wegrich. 2019. "Generalists and Specialists in Executive Politics: Why Ambitious Meta-Policies so Often Fail." *Public Administration* 97 (4): 845–60.

Jugl, Marlene. 2019. "Finding the Golden Mean: Country Size and the Performance of National Bureaucracies." *Journal of Public Administration Research and Theory* 29 (1): 118–32.

2020a. "Country Size and State Performance: How Size Affects Politics, Administration and Governance." Doctoral dissertation, Berlin: Hertie School. https://doi.org/10.48462/opus4-3680

2020b. "Public Administration in Small European States: Size, Characteristics and Performance." In *Handbook of Governance in Small States*, edited by Lino Briguglio, Jessica Byron, Stefano Moncada, and Wouter Veenendaal, 77–88. London: Routledge.

Jugl, Marlene, Wouter Veenendaal, Jack Corbett, and Roannie Ng Shiu. 2021. "How Does Population Size Influence Administrative Performance?" *Manuscript* 1–21.

Jung, Chan Su. 2013. "Navigating a Rough Terrain of Public Management: Examining the Relationship between Organizational Size and Effectiveness." *Journal of Public Administration Research and Theory* 23 (3): 663–86.

Jung, Chan Su, and Seok Eun Kim. 2014. "Structure and Perceived Performance in Public Organizations." *Public Management Review* 16 (5): 620–42.

Katzenstein, Peter J. 1985. *Small States in World Markets: Industrial Policy in Europe*. Ithaca: Cornell University Press.

Kaufmann, Daniel, Aart Kraay, and Massimo Mastruzzi. 2009. "Governance Matters VIII. Aggregate and Individual Governance Indicators 1996–2008." Policy Research Working Paper No. 4978. Washington, DC: World Bank.

Kettl, Donald F. 2020. "States Divided: The Implications of American Federalism for COVID-19." *Public Administration Review* 80 (4): 595–602.

Kickert, Walter J. M. 2011. "Public Management Reform in Continental Europe: National Distinctiveness." In *The Ashgate Research Companion to New Public Management*, edited by Tom Christensen and Per Lægreid, 97–112. Farnham, Burlington: Aahgate.

Kiser, Edgar, and Justin Baer. 2005. "The Bureaucratization of States: Toward an Analytical Weberianism." In *Remaking Modernity: Politics, History, and Sociology*, edited by Julia Adams, Elisabeth S. Clemens, and Ann S. Orloff, 225–46. Durham, NC: Duke University Press.

Kiser, Edgar, and Joachim Schneider. 1994. "Bureaucracy and Efficiency: An Analysis of Taxation in Early Modern Prussia." *American Sociological Review* 59 (2): 187–204.

Knack, Stephen, and Omar Azfar. 2000. "Are Larger Countries Really More Corrupt?" Policy Research Working Paper No. 2470. Washington, DC: The World Bank.

Kuhlmann, Sabine, and Hellmut Wollmann. 2014. *Introduction to Comparative Public Administration: Administrative Systems and Reforms in Europe.* Cheltenham: Edward Elgar.

Kurtz, Marcus J., and Andrew Schrank. 2007. "Growth and Governance: Models, Measures, and Mechanisms." *Journal of Politics* 69 (2): 538–54.

La Porta, Rafael, Florencio Lopez-de-Silanes, Andrei Shleifer, and Robert Vishny. 1999. "The Quality of Government." *Journal of Law, Economics, and Organization* 15 (1): 222–79.

Langbein, Laura, and Stephen Knack. 2010. "The Worldwide Governance Indicators: Six, One, or None?" *The Journal of Development Studies* 46 (2): 350–70.

Lewis, John P. 1991. "Some Consequences of Giantism: The Case of India." *World Politics* 43 (3): 367–89.

Lowenthal, David. 1987. "Social Features." In *Politics, Security and Development in Small States*, edited by Colin Clarke and Tony Payne, 26–49. London: Allen & Unwin.

Mann, Laura, and Marie Berry. 2016. "Understanding the Political Motivations That Shape Rwanda's Emergent Developmental State." *New Political Economy* 21 (1): 119–44.

Mayntz, Renate, and Fritz W. Scharpf. 1975. *Policy-Making in the German Federal Bureaucracy.* Amsterdam: Elsevier.

McDonnell, Erin Metz. 2017. "Patchwork Leviathan: How Pockets of Bureaucratic Governance Flourish within Institutionally Diverse Developing States." *American Sociological Review* 82 (3): 476–510.

Meer, Frits M. van der. 2018. "The Netherlands." Public Administration Characteristics and Performance in EU28. Brussels: European Commission. https://op.europa.eu/en/publication-detail/-/publication/e49ce32b-9605-11e8-8bc1-01aa75ed71a1/language-en

Meier, Kenneth J., Amanda Rutherford, and Claudia N. Avellaneda. 2017. *Comparative Public Management: Why National, Environmental, and Organizational Context Matters*. Washington, DC: Georgetown University Press.

Mele, Valentina, and Paolo Belardinelli. 2019. "Mixed Methods in Public Administration Research: Selecting, Sequencing, and Connecting." *Journal of Public Administration Research and Theory* 29 (2): 334–47.

MFP. 2020. "Boîte à Outils Pour l'élaboration Du Programme de Travail." Luxembourg: Ministère de la Fonction Publique. https://fonction-publique.public.lu/dam-assets/fr/documentation/fonctionpublique/boite-outils-web.pdf

MIF. 2020. "2020 Ibrahim Index of African Governance (IIAG) Dataset." Mo Ibrahim Foundation. https://mo.ibrahim.foundation/iiag

Moynihan, Donald. 2018. "A Great Schism Approaching? Towards a Micro and Macro Public Administration." *Journal of Behavioral Public Administration* 1 (1): 1–8.

Moynihan, Donald, Pamela Herd, and Hope Harvey. 2015. "Administrative Burden: Learning, Psychological, and Compliance Costs in Citizen-State Interactions." *Journal of Public Administration Research and Theory* 25 (1): 43–69.

Neumann, Iver B., and Sieglinde Gstöhl. 2006. "Lilliputians in Gulliver's World?" In *Small States in International Relations*, edited by Christine Ingebritsen, Iver B. Neumann, Sieglinde Gstöhl, and Jessica Beyer, 3–36. Seattle [et al.]: University of Washington Press [et al.].

Nistotskaya, Marina, and Luciana Cingolani. 2016. "Bureaucratic Structure, Regulatory Quality, and Entrepreneurship in a Comparative Perspective: Cross-Sectional and Panel Data Evidence." *Journal of Public Administration Research and Theory* 26 (3): 519–34.

Nistotskaya, Marina, Stefan Dahlberg, Carl Dahlström, et al. 2020. *The QoG Expert Survey Dataset: Wave III*. University of Gothenburg: The Quality of Government Institute.

Norris, Pippa. 2009. "Democracy Time-series Data. Release 3.0, January 2009." Kennedy School of Government, Harvard University. www.hks.harvard.edu/fs/pnorris/Data/Data.htm

OECD. 2019. "Government at a Glance 2019." Paris: OECD.

2021. "Government at a Glance 2021." Paris: OECD.

Olsson, Ola, and Gustav Hansson. 2011. "Country Size and the Rule of Law: Resuscitating Montesquieu." *European Economic Review* 55 (5): 613–29.

Ongaro, Edoardo, Ting Gong, and Yijia Jing. 2021. "Public Administration, Context and Innovation: A Framework of Analysis." *Public Administration and Development* 41(1): 4–114–11.

Ostrom, Elinor. 1972. "Metropolitan Reform: Propositions Derived from Two Traditions." *Social Science Quarterly* 53 (3): 474–93.

O'Toole Jr., Laurence J., and Kenneth J. Meier. 2014. "Public Management, Context, and Performance: In Quest of a More General Theory." *Journal of Public Administration Research and Theory* 25 (1): 237–56.

2017. "Introduction. Comparative Public Management: A Framework for Analysis." In *Comparative Public Management: Why National, Environmental, and Organizational Context Matters*, edited by Kenneth J. Meier, Amanda Rutherford, and Claudia N. Avellaneda, 1–26. Washington, DC: Georgetown University Press.

Painter, Martin, and B. Guy Peters. 2010. "Administrative Traditions in Comparative Perspective: Families, Groups and Hybrids." In *Tradition and Public Administration*, edited by Martin Painter and B. Guy Peters, 19–30. Basingstoke: Palgrave Macmillan.

Panke, Diana. 2010. *Small States in the European Union: Coping with Structural Disadvantages*. Farnham: Ashgate.

Pollitt, Christopher. 2011. "Not Odious but Onerous: Comparative Public Administration." *Public Administration* 89 (1): 114–27.

Pollitt, Christopher, and Geert Bouckaert. 2017. *Public Management Reform: A Comparative Analysis – Into the Age of Austerity*. 4th ed., Oxford: Oxford University Press.

Przeworski, Adam, and Henry Teune. 1970. *The Logic of Comparative Social Inquiry*. New York: Wiley.

Rainey, Hal G., and Chan Su Jung. 2015. "A Conceptual Framework for Analysis of Goal Ambiguity in Public Organizations." *Journal of Public Administration Research and Theory* 25 (1): 71–99.

Rainey, Hal G., and Paula Steinbauer. 1999. "Galloping Elephants: Developing Elements of a Theory of Effective Government Organizations." *Journal of Public Administration Research and Theory* 9 (1): 1–32.

Randma-Liiv, Tiina. 2002. "Small States and Bureaucracy: Challenges for Public Administration." *Trames* 6 (4): 374–89.

Randma-Liiv, Tiina, and Külli Sarapuu. 2019. "Public Governance in Small States: From Paradoxes to Research Agenda." In *A Research Agenda for Public Administration*, edited by Andrew Massey, 162–79. Cheltenham: Edward Elgar.

Rauch, James E., and Peter B. Evans. 2000. "Bureaucratic Structure and Bureaucratic Performance in Less Developed Countries." *Journal of Public Economics* 75 (1): 49–71.

Reichard, Christoph, and Eckhard Schröter. 2021. "Civil Service and Public Employment." In *Public Administration in Germany*, edited by Sabine Kuhlmann, Isabella Proeller, Dieter Schimanke, Jan Ziekow, 205–23. Cham: Palgrave Macmillan.

Roberts, Alasdair. 2020. "Bridging Levels of Public Administration: How Macro Shapes Meso and Micro." *Administration & Society* 52 (4): 631–56.

Rose, Andrew K. 2006. "Size Really Doesn't Matter: In Search of a National Scale Effect." *Journal of the Japanese and International Economies* 20 (4): 482–507.

Rothstein, Bo, and Jan Teorell. 2008. "What Is Quality of Government? A Theory of Impartial Government Institutions." *Governance* 21 (2): 165–90.

Sarapuu, Külli. 2010. "Comparative Analysis of State Administrations: The Size of State as an Independent Variable." *Halduskultuur – Administrative Culture* 11 (1): 30–43.

Sarapuu, Külli, and Tiina Randma-Liiv. 2020. "Small States: Public Management and Policy-Making." In *Handbook on the Politics of Small States*, edited by Godfrey Baldacchino and Anders Wivel, 55–69. Cheltenham: Edward Elgar.

Scharpf, Fritz W. 1988. "The Joint Decision Trap: Lessons from German Federalism and European Integration." *Public Administration* 66 (3): 239–78.

SGI. 2020. "Interministerial Coordination Report." Sustainable Governance Indicators 2020. Bertelsmann Foundation. https://www.sgi-network.org /docs/2020/thematic/SGI2020_Interministerial_Coordination.pdf

Slater, Dan, and Daniel Ziblatt. 2013. "The Enduring Indispensability of the Controlled Comparison." *Comparative Political Studies* 46 (10): 1301–27.

Snijders, Tom A. B., and Roel J. Bosker. 1999. *Multilevel Analysis: An Introduction to Basic and Advanced Multilevel Modeling*. 1st ed. London: SAGE.

Stevenson, Angus, ed. 2015. *Oxford Dictionary of English*. 3rd ed., online version. Oxford: Oxford University Press.

Streeten, Paul. 1993. "The Special Problems of Small Countries." *World Development* 21 (2): 197–202.

Sutton, Paul. 1987. "Political Aspects." In *Politics, Security and Development in Small States*, edited by Colin Clarke and Tony Payne, 3–25. London: Allen & Unwin.

Taylor, Charles L. 1969. "Statistical Typology of Micro-States and Territories." *Social Science Information* 8 (3): 101–17.

Thijs, Nick, Gerhard Hammerschmid, and Enora Palaric. 2018. "A Comparative Overview of Public Administration Characteristics and Performance in EU28." European Commission, 1–104. https://op.europa.eu/en/publication-detail/-/publication/3e89d981-48fc-11e8-be1d-01aa75ed71a1/language-en

Thorhallsson, Baldur. 2000. *The Role of Small States in the European Union.* Aldershot: Ashgate.

2006. "The Size of States in the European Union: Theoretical and Conceptual Perspectives." *European Integration* 28 (1): 7–31.

Toonen, Theo A. J. 2007. "Administrative Reform: Analytics." In *Handbook of Public Administration: Concise Paperback Edition*, edited by B. Guy Peters and Jon Pierre, 301–10. London: SAGE.

Toshkov, Dimiter, Kutsal Yesilkagit, and Brendan Carroll. 2021. "Government Capacity, Societal Trust or Party Preferences? What Accounts for the Variety of National Policy Responses to the COVID-19 Pandemic in Europe?" *Journal of European Public Policy.* Online first: 1–20.

Treisman, Daniel. 2007. *The Architecture of Government: Rethinking Political Decentralization.* New York: Cambridge University Press.

Tullock, Gordon. 1969. "Federalism: Problems of Scale." *Public Choice* 6 (1): 19–29.

Urwick, Lyndall. 2003 [1937]. "Organization as a Technical Problem." In *Papers on the Science of Administration*, edited by Luther Gulick and Lyndall Urwick, Reprint, 50–96. London: Routledge.

Veenendaal, Wouter P. 2014. *Politics and Democracy in Microstates.* London: Routledge.

2020. "When Things Get Personal: How Informal and Personalized Politics Produce Regime Stability in Small States." *Government and Opposition* 55(3): 393–412.

Veenendaal, Wouter P., and Jack Corbett. 2015. "Why Small States Offer Important Answers to Large Questions." *Comparative Political Studies* 48 (4): 527–49.

Wal, Zeger van der, Caspar van den Berg, and M. Shamsul Haque. 2021. "Comparative Public Administration in a Globalized World: Moving Beyond Standard Assumptions towards Increased Understanding." *Public Administration Review* 81(2): 295–98.

Walker, Richard M., George A. Boyne, and Gene A. Brewer. 2010. "Introduction." In *Public Management and Performance. Research Directions*, edited by Richard M. Walker, George A. Boyne, and Gene A. Brewer, 1–33. Cambridge: Cambridge University Press.

Walle, Steven van de. 2006. "The State of the World's Bureaucracies." *Journal of Comparative Policy Analysis: Research and Practice* 8 (4): 437–48.

Weber, Max. 1978 [1922]. *Economy and Society.* Edited by Guenther Roth and Claus Wittich. 5th ed. 2 vols. Berkeley: University of California Press.

Wegrich, Kai. 2021. "Is the Turtle Still Plodding along? Public Management Reform in Germany." *Public Management Review* 23 (8): 1107–16.

Wegrich, Kai, and Gerhard Hammerschmid. 2018. "Germany." Public Administration Characteristics and Performance in EU28. Brussels: European Commission.

Williamson, Oliver E. 1967. "Hierarchical Control and Optimum Firm Size." *Journal of Political Economy* 75 (2): 123–38.

Wilson, James Q. 1989. *Bureaucracy: What Government Agencies Do and Why They Do It.* New York: Basic Books.

Xin, Xiaohui, and Thomas K. Rudel. 2004. "The Context for Political Corruption: A Cross-National Analysis." *Social Science Quarterly* 85 (2): 294–309.

Yasuda, John Kojiro. 2015. "Why Food Safety Fails in China: The Politics of Scale." *The China Quarterly* 223: 745–69.

Yesilkagit, Kutsal, and Sandra Van Thiel. 2012. "The Netherlands." In *Government Agencies: Practices and Lessons from 30 Countries*, edited by Koen Verhoest, Sandra Van Thiel, Geert Bouckaert, and Per Lægreid, 179–90. Public Sector Organizations. Basingstoke [et al.]: Palgrave Macmillan.

Ziller, Jacques. 2007. "The Continental System of Administrative Legality." In *Handbook of Public Administration: Concise Paperback Edition*, edited by B. Guy Peters and Jon Pierre, 167–75. London: SAGE.

Acknowledgments

This Element would not have been possible without the support of several scholars who have continuously encouraged me to pursue my research interests and who provided helpful advice since I embarked on the topic of country size in 2015 as a doctoral student in Berlin. First of all, I thank Jack Corbett for encouraging me to write this Element. I am also grateful to Tony Bertelli for continuous encouragement and strategic advice over the last years. Parts of this Element are based on an article published in JPART and on my doctoral dissertation. In particular, the analyses in Section 4 are based on the earlier article, and Mark Kayser provided valuable comments on an earlier version of that article. I thank Kai Wegrich for his constructive supervision of my doctoral research and his generous support. Finally, I thank Francesca Squillante for excellent research assistance and Rebecca Kirley and a reviewer for helpful suggestions and comments on an earlier draft.

Cambridge Elements ≡

Public and Nonprofit Administration

Andrew Whitford
University of Georgia
Andrew Whitford is Alexander M. Crenshaw Professor of Public Policy in the School of Public and International Affairs at the University of Georgia. His research centers on strategy and innovation in public policy and organization studies.

Robert Christensen
Brigham Young University
Robert Christensen is professor and George Romney Research Fellow in the Marriott School at Brigham Young University. His research focuses on prosocial and antisocial behaviors and attitudes in public and nonprofit organizations.

About the Series
The foundation of this series are cutting-edge contributions on emerging topics and definitive reviews of keystone topics in public and nonprofit administration, especially those that lack longer treatment in textbook or other formats. Among keystone topics of interest for scholars and practitioners of public and nonprofit administration, it covers public management, public budgeting and finance, nonprofit studies, and the interstitial space between the public and nonprofit sectors, along with theoretical and methodological contributions, including quantitative, qualitative and mixed-methods pieces.

The Public Management Research Association
The Public Management Research Association improves public governance by advancing research on public organizations, strengthening links among interdisciplinary scholars, and furthering professional and academic opportunities in public management.

Cambridge Elements ≡

Public and Nonprofit Administration

Elements in the Series

A full series listing is available at: www.cambridge.org/EPNP

Printed in the United States
by Baker & Taylor Publisher Services